CHESAPEAKE ODYSSEYS

CHESAPEAKE ODYSSEYS

An 1883 Cruise Revisited

BY JOSEPH T. ROTHROCK, M. D.
AND JANE C. ROTHROCK
WITH PHOTOGRAPHS BY JOSEPH T. ROTHROCK III

TIDEWATER   PUBLISHERS
Centreville, Maryland

Library of Congress Cataloging in Publication Data

Rothrock, Joseph T., 1839-1922.
    Chesapeake odysseys.

    1. Chesapeake Bay (Md. and Va.)—Description and
travel. 2. Natural history—Chesapeake Bay (Md. and Va.)
3. Yachts and yachting—Chesapeake Bay (Md. and Va.)
4. Rothrock, Joseph T., 1839-1922. 5. Rothrock, Jane C.,
1948-   . I. Rothrock, Jane C., 1948-   .
II. Title.
F187.C5R67   1984   917.55′180441   84-40343
ISBN 0-87033-323-2

Manufactured in the United States of America
First edition

To My Mother
This little volume is affectionately dedicated,
in grateful remembrance of her devotion
to the well-being and happiness of her children.
　　　　　　　　　—J. T. Rothrock, M. D.

To the Memory of Our Mothers
Knowing how they would have rejoiced
at our undertaking this project
both inspired and encouraged us.
　　　　　　　　　—Jane C. and Joseph T. Rothrock III

Contents

Publisher's Preface

IN June 1883 Joseph T. Rothrock, M.D., set forth on his thirty-four-foot sloop *Martha* with a plan to spend a vacation cruising, studying, and photographing the natural history of Chesapeake Bay. What became a delightful three-month sailing odyssey began on the Chesapeake and Delaware Canal. It meandered from the mouth of the Elk River in Maryland southward to the James River in Virginia, traversed the James up and back, and finally crisscrossed the Bay several times before returning to the original point of departure. Bending to the dictates of the weather or the fascination of locale, Dr. Rothrock made many stopovers along the rivers and coves of the Bay. Here the vacationing scientist indulged his interest in fossil remains, geological formations, and early American settlements.

An account of this cruise, the most significant part of which was about Chesapeake Bay, and is reprinted here, was published in 1884 by J. B. Lippincott and entitled *Vacation Cruising in Chesapeake and Delaware Bays*. Dr. Rothrock was a practicing physician and eminent botanist at the University of Pennsylvania, who later formulated the policy of forest conservation for the state of Pennsylvania. In this warm, engaging narrative, he revealed himself predominantly as a concerned scientist—concerned about all aspects of the human condition. The inhuman ravages of the Civil War still evident in Virginia engrossed him, and the urgent need for conservation of the nation's natural resources permeated his thought and outlook.

9

Publisher's Preface

In June 1983, Dr. Rothrock's great-grandson Joseph T. Rothrock III, and his wife, Jane, retraced that memorable cruise in their twenty-six-foot, British-built sailboat *Response*. Their purpose was twofold: to fulfill a sense of family tradition (in their home they had Dr. Rothrock's 1884 book, his many original photographs, and the camera with which he so dutifully documented his trip); and to satisfy their own curiosity to see what changes would be revealed by a similar cruise one hundred years later.

In *Chesapeake Odysseys* Dr. Rothrock's original narrative is reproduced on the left-hand pages of the book while the 1983 voyage parallels it on the right-hand side. Similarly, the photographs taken a century ago are arranged with their modern counterparts. The placement of text and pictures in this way enables the reader to follow both voyages readily and to enjoy the benefit of historical perspective.

Preface

MANY of us, if we took the time, could probably find things in our family histories that would fascinate or intrigue us. The Rothrock family, being one that keeps its treasures alive for each generation to inspect, simply made us more aware of family history earlier on in our lives. We did not *have* to be fascinated with it, but it so happened that we were.

There are strong parallels in the interests of the Rothrocks throughout the years; boating is one that has permeated the existence of us all. The desire, then, to read great-grandfather's 1884 volume, *Vacation Cruising in Chesapeake and Delaware Bays*, was simply an extension of our natural interests and our love of the Bay.

The idea of following his cruise, made in 1883, did not occur to us right away. Over the years we would make reference to his having been in the same part of the Bay in which we found ourselves, but this was done in the context of an idle comment. It wasn't until we began thinking about our vacation plans for 1983 that the thought struck us that it would be exactly a hundred years since he had wandered down and written about the Bay; in that context, a centennial celebration of sorts, we saw the making of the same cruise as a very logical and exciting thing to do with our summer.

So we did.

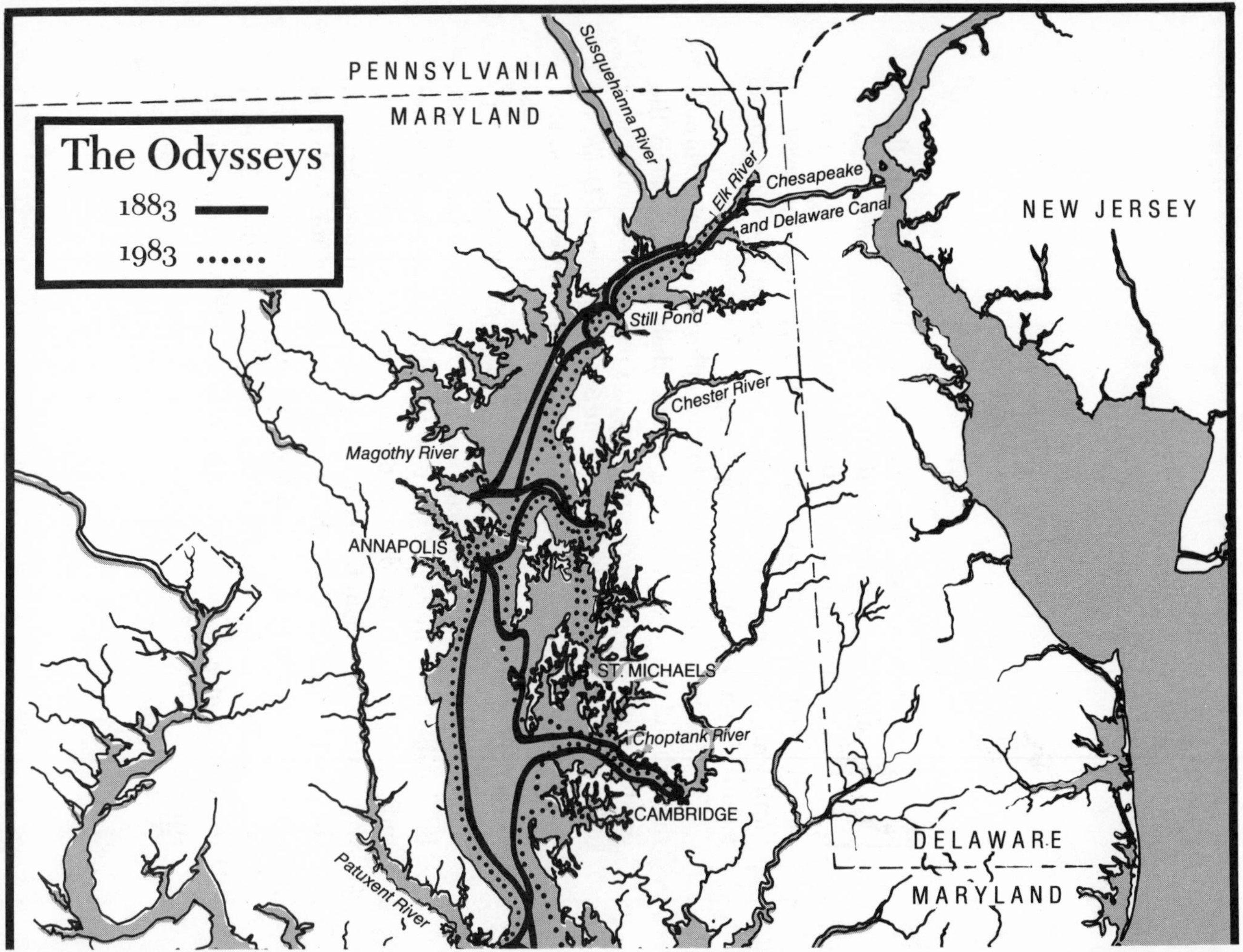
The Odysseys
1883
1983
PENNSYLVANIA
MARYLAND
Susquehanna River
Elk River
Chesapeake
and Delaware Canal
NEW JERSEY
Still Pond
Chester River
Magothy River
ANNAPOLIS
ST. MICHAELS
Choptank River
CAMBRIDGE
Patuxent River
DELAWARE
MARYLAND

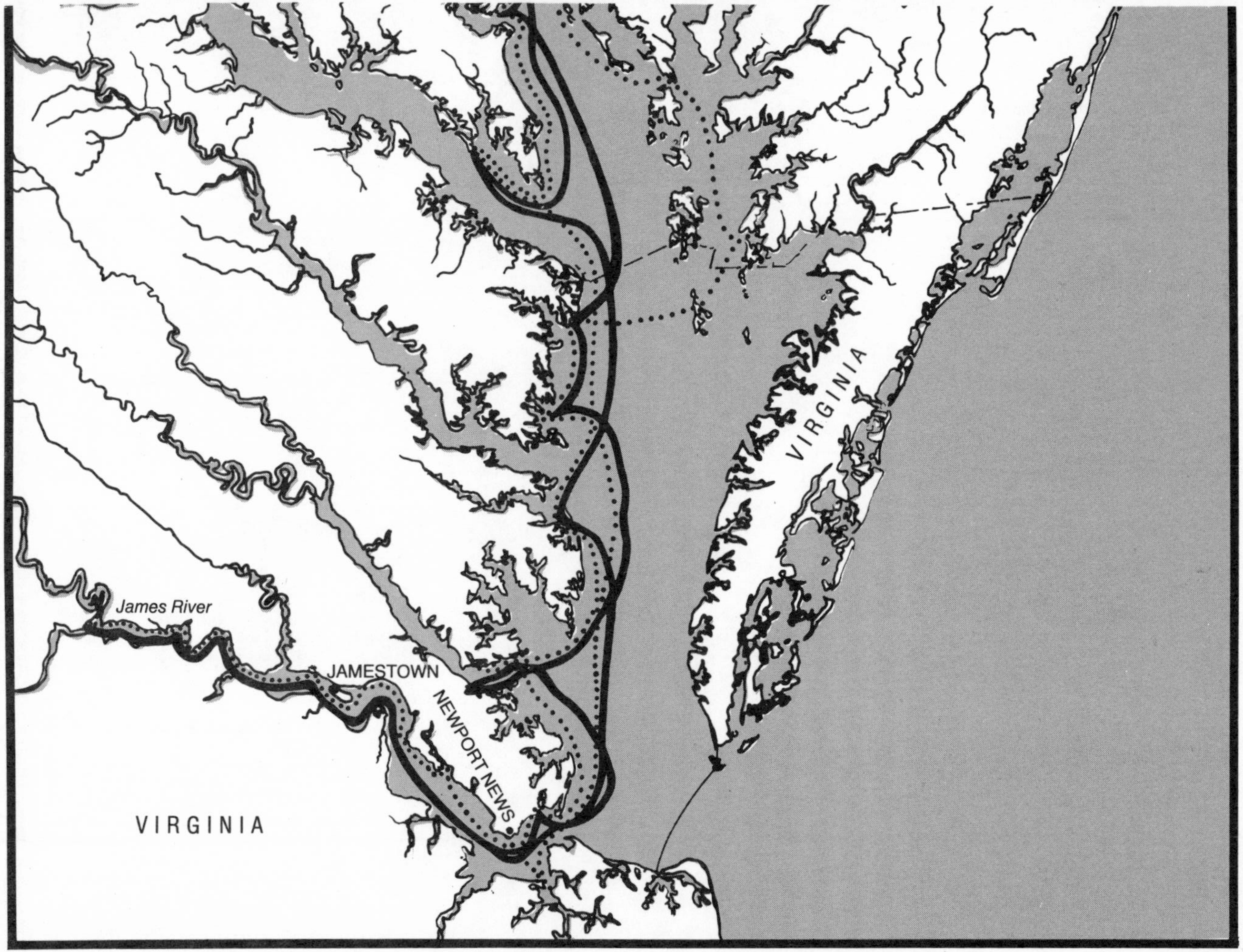
James River
JAMESTOWN
NEWPORT NEWS
VIRGINIA
VIRGINIA

CHESAPEAKE ODYSSEYS

CHAPTER I.

DESCRIPTION OF THE YACHT, AND REASONS FOR THE CRUISE.

THE plan of spending this vacation on the water grew gradually, and at last commended itself to my judgment, because it was cheap, full of health, and promised as complete a change in mode of life as one could hope to obtain.

Furthermore, as I proposed partly utilizing the time by such natural history studies and observations as would not consume brain-power faster than it was created, some few books, a microscope, plant-press, and paper were required. These conditions were most fully met by making a small yacht my means of conveyance, my home, and my laboratory. It is to be remembered that study was far from being the primary object of the cruise.

To carry out my plan a strong, nearly new boat was purchased, —not a racing yacht, in which everything was sacrificed to speed, but a solid, "well-fastened" little sloop, whose qualities were safety first, comfort second, and some speed at the tail-end of a long list of good points.

The custom-house papers gave thirty feet long, eleven feet beam, and three and a half feet deep as the dimensions of the little craft. Much greater depth and less beam in proportion to length are now regarded as important elements of safety, and doubtless truly so; but I was obliged to have a boat whose depth would not prevent my entering harbors where I particularly desired to go. An old waterman expressed his opinion of my boat "Martha" by saying, "You can't drown her."

No more sail was carried than was absolutely required. The spars were shorter and stronger than were usual in sloops of her

16

Chapter 1

OUR plan to follow great-grandfather's vacation/working cruise of 1883 grew in our minds during the fall and winter of 1982. We found ourselves voraciously buying books about the Chesapeake so that we might augment our meager knowledge. Our most important source for this work came, however, from great-grandfather's 1884 book itself. We read the book in earnest, mapping out his ports of call, and, tentatively, his anchorages. We decided to establish our plans on his detailed account of his own voyage. To our surprise and delight, the book was extremely helpful. We were relieved that we would not be attempting to undertake a scientific research project nor charting buoys and compass headings. Therefore, we decided our cruise should take place in the month of June, 1983.

Early in the spring we began to spend weekends at our home berth in Higgins Yacht Yard, St. Michaels, Maryland. As anyone who has ever been involved in readying a boat for the sailing season knows, excitement and pleasure mount with each new activity. That year these reactions were even more intense than usual. Our boat *Response* is documented as twenty-six feet in length, with an eight-foot beam and three-and-a-half-foot draft. She is British-built, solid, and maneuverable, with twin keels that achieve steadiness even at the cost of speed. In spite of being a small boat, she has a cabin that provides enough room to make a comfortable home on board. There is plenty of storage space for the provisions and accessories that accompany a cruise. Commissioned thirteen years ago, she is kept in a condition that we

The "Martha"

size; and, as further security against a capsize, more than a ton of
pig iron was placed and fastened as low down inside as we could
get it. Six hundred to a thousand pounds more outside on her keel
would have added to her sailing qualities, though without this the
boat gave no indication of unsteadiness.

Before the vacation began every seam had been most carefully
gone over and made tight; the standing rigging was newly set up,
and every cord of the running rigging was either new, or as good as
new. Our ground tackle was two powerful holding anchors and
plenty of manila rope to swing to. Cleats and reefing gear were all
in perfect order. Not once during the entire summer were we
endangered or incommoded from want of preparation of anything
we should have had ready, but which was not ready.

18

The *Response*

describe as "nearly new," which really means she is safe, sound, clean, and homey.

Outfitting a boat for a bay cruise can be as simple or as complex as the boater desires it to be. But, as far as we are concerned, convenience and efficiency are the main qualities we require of a boat. Therefore, we did not want more sails than were absolutely necessary; we had a roller-furling jib, and added only a cruising spinnaker with a self-dousing sock to the main for sail power. Of course, we also carried a "Chesapeake Bay mainsail," known to nonbay boaters as a sunshade. We considered this a required piece of gear because we pride ourselves on achieving simplicity without giving up comfort. We are not willing to compromise on safety either. This is why weekends spent in getting ready, with

19

A good aneroid barometer held a place so conspicuous that it *must* be noticed, and thus we were left without excuse if not forewarned of coming danger by storm. Compass, charts, and lead and line, side-lights, anchor-light, and cabin-light completed the details that contemplated safety.

Next came comfort. First of all, every avenue to the cabin was guarded by wire mosquito-netting,—so well guarded that we absolutely escaped all torments from these minute flying fiends. We always kept the sliding cabin windows open. Hence, we had the full benefit by day and by night of whatever "air was going." The "bunks" were large enough for men of moderate dimensions to sleep comfortably in, with tossing room besides. The rule that all bedding must be frequently aired was religiously adhered to.

For food, canned corn, tomatoes, and baked beans, with rice, oatmeal, prunes, good pilot-bread, ham and the best breakfast bacon, tea, coffee, and sugar, I purchased for the season at whole-sale price. Fresh fruits and meats were obtained as required. If there was lack of luxurious living, there was no want of nutritious plain food. The medicine-case was well supplied,—not that it was needed much for the inmates of the boat, but because, in out-of-the-way places where we went, it often enabled me to relieve some suffering fellow. There is comfort in giving help without hope of reward, or without possibility of it, save such mental approval as a pure charity brings to the giver. A little of this does go a long way into after-life, softening one's own sorrows, and brightening his own joys. Hence, then, by all means, a medicine-chest.

Another most important article was added—a small, cheap camera for dry-plate photography. One may now be had at a price which is within reach of every tourist, and nothing is easier than to become an adept in the use of the instrument. Let me suggest, however, that each tourist contemplating a prolonged trip pur-chase enough plates at once for his use, and that he fairly test their sensitiveness before leaving his base of supplies. I have no com-plaints to make because a large proportion of the plates of a well-known dealer failed to give the results I had anticipated, and

the back-up help from a knowledgeable boatyard crew to guide
and direct our efforts, resulted in our being able to get where we
planned to go without risk or delay.

Since there is always danger in sailing the bay in a small craft,
we carried both barometer and VHF radio. When the barometer
began to indicate an approaching storm, we were quick to tune in
our radio to a weather station in order to obtain predictions for our
area. A radio provides the cruising sailor with several kinds of
communication, and although we found it most useful for de-
termining weather and for talking with other sailing vessels, we
also found it indispensable simply for its listening value. Knowing
that help is a radio call away does not insure against trouble, but it
certainly does ensure peace of mind.

A compass and charts complemented the radio and barometer
in outfitting the *Response*. To replace lead and line as a way of
determing what lay beneath us, we installed a depth finder unit
that did all but direct our course! This particular unit also provided a knot meter and trip log along with its programmable
alarm, allowing us to set our warning depth according to the
waters we were in. With the information on our charts, we were
aided both in keeping off the bottom and in keeping on course. As
a navigational aid, our depth finder has two built-in alarms; one
alarm beeps slowly to warn that the bottom is gradually shoaling,
while the other beeps quickly to warn that the bottom is going to
be contacted if someone doesn't immediately man the tiller. Since
we had gotten into the habit of giving our technological assistants
affectionate names, the depth finder soon became DF—dear
friend.

In order to break the monotony of sitting long hours at the
helm on a windless day, we decided to install an additional accessory. It was called an autohelm by the manufacturer. We dubbed
this piece of equipment the AH—almighty hand. Battery driven,
it was seated quietly on deck with us, steering the tiller by the
compass heading we dialed in. Our AH was never the only hand on
deck, but it did take its turn at the helm in both calm and
somewhat rough seas, under sail or motor. Its efficiency surprised

which I had always obtained before from his supplies. The fault was my own, that I had not tried the lot before starting out. We can hardly as yet guess how important a factor this amateur photography is to be in the book-making of the future. Neither can we measure its possible influence in opening minds to the quiet beauty or the sublime grandeur which our land everywhere possesses. To judge what its possible effect may be a century hence, study what it has already done for men—and women too—who, before they became amateurs, had no appreciation of the fact that a tree or a rock could have either individuality or attractiveness. Without wishing to be over-enthusiastic, or be regarded as filled with the zeal of a neophyte, I can hardly avoid counting this art in as one of the humanizing forces of the times.

For reading matter, what so good as some of Kingsley's writings? Real enough to charm and invigorate the mind, suggestive enough to open whole realms to any student who has the capacity for observation or for generalization, yet without the details with which some authors drag their readers down to the level of those everlasting figures. There is a mental condition which grows out of constantly contemplating ratio and percentage which is dangerous, because the victim always fails to notice that the sunshine is leaving his soul, and that, as his facts and his averages pile themselves higher and higher, his own inner self is being dwarfed. Who of all writers could so fitly fill the little space left for reading matter as Charles Kingsley? Of course there were, besides, the ordinary scientific and yachting manuals.

Who should go cruising? There is a constantly-increasing number of young and middle-aged men who, under the exactions of daily duty, find themselves each spring physically below par. Many of them cannot afford the cost of a prolonged trip by the ordinary means of travel, even if it be undertaken in the interest of health. Indeed, it is by no means certain that such a vacation would yield the largest return, for the simple reason that there is nothing for the individual to do, save to pay his bills and be taken care of. Thus the stimulus of personal activity and of responsibility is missed, and with it, also, that complete change in mental

us, and its cost seemed inconsequential after we had sailed with it
for five weeks.

Although we did not wish to make comfort and convenience
the chief prerequisites for a happy sojourn, we did consider it
essential to make certain concessions. Thus we brought aboard
soft, stowable mosquito netting with velcro stripping, mosquito
coils, and citronella candles for protection from the bugs, as well
as windscoops and fans for protection from the heat. The notions
of comfort haven't changed in one hundred years, only the manner by which comfort is provided. The accoutrements of comfort
can be elaborated upon in some yachts so that air conditioning,
hot running water, microwave ovens, even bathtubs appear on
the list. On the *Response* we managed splendidly with sun showers, the hot water from which bathed our bodies and whatever
else we needed to wash. We did indulge ourselves to the extent of
carrying a small, battery-operated television and radio, hooked as
we are on classical music and the "Prairie Home Companion."
Add to the list a green plant, fresh flowers when in port, and the
many dimensions of comfort were satisfactorily met as far as we
were concerned.

Reading matter is an individual preference that is reflected no
less in the books taken aboard than in those found in the home
library. Compulsive mystery readers, we had a plentiful supply of
Christie, Le Carré, and Conan Doyle. We also stocked Miche-
ner's novels. We found a number of marinas with book trading
centers, so that we were well supplied with fresh reading material
when we wanted it. Of course, we had the nursing and photo-
graphic journals and yachting books to satisfy our professional and
boating interests.

There are many galley cookbooks on the market today to
enhance meal preparation on board. We are committed to the
concepts of good nutrition and convenience while enjoying variety. Anything fresh was preferred, and meal planning was aimed
at supplying small portions, to be easily prepared and attractively
served, with no waste or leftovers. The charcoal grill was a favored
way of doing fish, fowl, or beef, although it must be admitted that,

occupation which a cruise is sure to afford, if it be such as I have tried to describe.

The essential substratum upon which health must rest is muscular exertion. Muscular fibre comes only when earned. However valuable as aids, I doubt whether all the tonics of the shops, alone, ever created an ounce of muscle. Cruising affords not only the incentive to, but the opportunity for, healthful exercise.

Who should not go cruising? First, those who expect nothing but comfort, and who cannot endure plain living, or those to whom monotonous drifting one day, with possibly a tempest-tossing the next, is a greater annoyance than a week of pleasant sailing and free, open-air life can compensate for. Second, those *whose education has been so neglected* that they have never been taught to enjoy exposure for the manhood which it brings.

There is a third class who should not go cruising. I mean such as enjoy being weak,—those creatures to whom bronzed skins and excessive vitality are an abomination. To such we would say, Stay at home, by all means! In the whole world out of doors there is no place for you.

Within a few years "the canoe" has awakened a profound interest in the United States. The constantly-increasing number of those who yield each summer to the fascination of the paddle shows that there must be, as we know there is, infinite pleasure in skimming our inland waters. Nothing that has been written in advocacy of yachting is to be construed as against "canoeing." They belong together as forms of the same recreation, each having its sphere, and each yielding a full return for the time and money expended, providing discretion rules the individual.

Caution: *Cruising in fresh water, remember your quinine-bottle. In the South, whether on fresh or salt water, keep in mind the same injunction.*

One more element remained to be considered, which, if not under the head of comfort, comes under the more important one of health,—I mean cleanliness. Nothing so disturbs rest as the thought that as one sleeps visitors, demons of the night, children of filth, are feasting upon his blood; or that some disease-germ,

in part, it was because the grill got us out of the cabin more, and fostered sharing the cooking chores, rather than its healthful aspects, that made it so popular on our boat.

Because we were interested in duplicating some of the foods carried by great-grandfather, to satisfy our notions of romance and authenticity, we spent a little time researching pilot bread. With the assistance of Mrs. William Portlock of the Sargent Memorial Room, Norfolk Public Library, a definition from the *Dictionary of Gastronomy* revealed that pilot wafers or crackers meant hardtack. We were further enlightened with information found in *Wilderness Cooking* which gives a description of hardtack as flat bread, often favored by the early settlers and scouts because it was easy to carry on long trips in the wilderness and at the same time was almost weightless. As dried round cakes, hardtack could be carried for months on end without getting stale. Hardtack could be used as a complement to any food where soft bread was normally used. Or, it could be softened in water and then boiled to make a palatable porridge which when cooled could be mixed with wild berries. Served with milk in a bowl, this was an easy dish to prepare.

This recipe, taken from a one hundred and sixty year old handwritten cookbook, makes a satisfactory bread, good in flavor, and nourishing:

> 2 cups graham flour
> 2 teaspoons salt
> 1 teaspoon soda
> 1 cup lard, melted
> 2 cups buttermilk
> white flour

In a large mixing bowl blend the graham flour, salt, and soda. Add the boiling hot lard to the mixture and stir well. Add the buttermilk, which should be at room temperature. Knead the dough in enough flour to make it hard enough to roll paper thin. Place on top of the stove to cook, or use a heavy pancake griddle.

vigorous in the absence of fumigation, is nursing in his veins a progeny that shall work him unknown harm. This bar to bliss when cruising is often intimately associated with a hired vessel. But then there could be no excuse for it on board one's own yacht, so I determined that, inside and out, the vessel should be cleaned every day. This rule was observed during the entire cruise, save for two weeks very early in the season. The yacht was also pumped out, washed out, and fumigated on the least suspicion that anything might be wrong, or on the bare idea that peace of mind or health of body could be in the least degree subserved by any additional precaution.

And now,—

> Over the rail
> My hand I trail,
> Within the shadow of the sail;
> A joy intense,
> The cooling sense
> Glides down my drowsy indolence.
> —*Drifting.*

Each piece should be a ten-inch circle with a center hole. The bread will bake in a short time. Remove it from the stove and allow to dry completely.

We carried with us any number of cameras, rolls of film, and even some processing apparatus. Preferring to be safe rather than sorry, we were prepared for any contingency and, consequently, met none. People often asked us what camera we would recommend for them to use, and invariably our expert photographer would suggest something reasonably priced and easy to use. The cameras were always accessible in the cabin when we were under way, as were the binoculars, so that we would not miss the opportunity of looking closely at or recording the things that enchanted or intrigued us.

Thus it was that we set out a century later to document by word and by picture an inherited agenda for making a vacation cruise on the Chesapeake.

CHAPTER II.

DOWN THE CHESAPEAKE AND UP THE JAMES.

FRIDAY afternoon, June 9, I met the "Martha" at Delaware City, whence we were to go through the canal to the Chesapeake Bay. Of course it was an unlucky day to begin a long trip, though I am bound to declare that, looking back on the events of the cruise, I do not see just where the misfortunes came in. The day was exceedingly warm, and a dead calm rested upon the waters. The glare of the sun was almost intolerable to the eyes; though I must say here that this intolerance of the bright reflection ceased in a few days.

The hours from ten, when I reached the place, until three, when the yacht came into the lock, passed away very slowly. The local industry which appeared to be most thriving at that time was sturgeon-catching. Two or three antiquated river sloops and schooners lay alongside the wharf. The odor arising from them told plainly enough what their vocation was. But the crews of these sturgeon-boats revealed most unexpectedly a fondness for the beautiful. The air of the town was filled with the perfume of roses, which were then blooming in profusion. Sturdy, oil-odored sturgeon-fishermen wandered through the town with huge clusters of roses, giving you as they passed the mingled perfume of the rose and the fish in the same inhalation. This unlooked for susceptibility, however, was not so strange as it was to discover that the place where the roses came from was a bar-room filled with a noisy crowd. The roses and the rye were dispensed over the same bar.

The "Martha" entered the lock at Delaware City, as has been said, at three in the afternoon. By four we were hitched on to the

Chapter 2

ONDAY morning, June 6th, we departed from St.
Michaels, heading for the Chesapeake and Delaware
Canal to begin our twentieth-century odyssey. Pulling
away from the dock at 6 A.M., the *Response* made way quietly out
of the channel, past sleeping crews that could not know the
delight with which we were anticipating the beginning of our
cruise. To leave so early in the morning, with the dawn still
unbroken, is like slipping away in secrecy. The excitement that
accompanies the start of a journey took hold of us, and nothing
could suppress the joy we felt. We had begun.

It was an easy stopover by dinghy from an anchorage in the public
basin to the Chesapeake and Delaware Canal Museum. This was a
necessary visit for us because we wanted to be historically accu-
rate. It was time well spent. We learned that the reason for the
canal's existence was really very simple; it allowed a boat, such as
ours and great-grandfather's, to pass from the Delaware Bay into
the Chesapeake Bay without having to travel around Cape
Charles. The very need for expediency, which underlined the
necessity for this canal, is probably what put many other canals
out of business in the late 1800s. As railroad tracks were laid, often
parallel to the waterways, the locomotives puffed their way into
providing a much speedier method of transportation. Many of the
canals in Pennsylvania were allowed to dry up. Overgrown beds
with crumbling canal houses are the only testimony to their once
vital existence. This was not the fate of the Chesapeake and

The canal locks at Chesapeake City

steam-tug "Swallow," and long before dark were through the canal.

As a rule, there is no inspiration in canal navigation, or certainly few people find it. For all this it was a really enjoyable trip across from bay to bay. Our transit was made in the delicious cool of the evening, after a frightfully hot day. The adjectives used are strictly intentional and premeditated, for the sufficient reason that they may express more truly than figures how the noonday and evening temperature affected us. I do not know where the mercury would have stood, because I never carry a thermometer when on a Southern cruise in summer, for it is simply exasperating to know just how much heat we are enduring. It is far more comfortable not to have the exact figures; they always intensify the

Delaware Canal, however. It is one of the busiest in the world today, connecting the ocean and coastal ports of Philadelphia and Baltimore. The locks which great-grandfather had to travel through have long since been removed and the canal widened to four hundred and fifty feet and deepened to thirty-five feet. The steam engines and lift wheel, enormous in size, are displayed in the museum; these engines drove the lift wheel which raised the water level, allowing the transit to be made. Told in this way, through exhibits and film, the canal's history impressed upon us more deeply than it would have otherwise how rapid the passage of time actually is. We left the museum with a better understanding of the significance of the canal as part of the Bay's heritage, as well as of the present-day operation of the canal.

We had often traveled on the Elk River, but never in the *Response*. For the past seven years, we had spent weekends along the Elk while attending the Eastern Shore Small Craft Institute camp, under the auspices of the Delaware division of the Red Cross. As a sailing instructor, Joe had taught classes in all levels of sailing. As a student, I had progressed through the courses, beginning with basic sailing. Thinking back on those years of learning how to sail, I remember how frightened I was when I first saw the shipping lanes through which we were now moving. To watch a passing merchant ship move slowly by, in the heavily traveled channel, brought back the initial feeling of dread I had had in my little Sunfish. Through the years, though, dread had turned into confidence, as I became more adept in handling a small boat. When I took intermediate and spinnaker sailing courses, I went past Elk Neck State Park into Rogues Harbor for practice in anchoring. In this little cove, at the foot of Elk Neck's high bluffs, I practiced that manuever, the actual operation of anchoring duly drilled into me by the crew. Afterwards, the class was offered lunch and a swim as rewards for completing the lesson. On the trip back to camp, we might review the aerodynamics of a sail. On other weekends, instruction took place in Cabin John Creek or on a short cruise to Turkey Point, where the lighthouse was incorporated into a discussion of aids to navigation.

31

Summit Bridge

sun's rays. In the canal we enjoyed the scenery and the rich perfume of the magnolia and the foxgrape. I would really like to spend a week in working (botanizing) along the banks of the canal. There is a luxuriant, and apparently a very varied, flora in the region.

On Saturday morning our patience was almost exhausted before we were taken in tow by the tug for the Elk River. The master of the tug did not care to venture out so long as the fog remained dense. Probably he was entirely right, because until eight o'clock objects distant more than a hundred yards were shut out from view; though the captain of a large Crisfield schooner did not think so, and, hoisting his sails, he started to work his way down to the Elk. However,—"luck in leisure,"—we passed him very soon when the tug did start.

As we entered the Elk the fog cleared away entirely, and the glorious water view opened before us to the southward. I never look from above the Bohemian River toward the bay that this

32

Summit Bridge

Before the wind, or on another point of sail determined by the
instructor, I learned—on the Elk River—to value the variety of
experiences sailing brings.

The area between the Chesapeake and Delaware Canal and the
Choptank is considered by some to provide the best cruising on
the Bay. To our minds, the whole of the Chesapeake is the sine
qua non for sailboat cruising. The shores are notched with river
mouths, which lead to coves and creeks and towns, offering
shelter and endless exploration. On the upper Eastern Shore,
Still Pond is among a number of attractive places that entice the
visiting yachter. It is certainly much better now, in terms of
accessibility, than it was for great-grandfather a hundred years
ago. The presence of a Coast Guard station inside the point on the
north shore undoubtedly accounts for the dredging that has gone
on there. While many of our sailing friends anchor outside, the
way in is fairly well marked, but it is tight—very tight. Inside,

panorama does not impress me. It does so more and more the oftener I look at and enjoy it. To the south there is no visible limit. The bold, timber-covered bluffs east or west, with navigable rivers coming in between, run so that the horizon widens as one looks south. It is a scene characterized neither by grandeur nor yet by quiet beauty alone. The combination of water, of plains, and of hills in just the proper proportion is what completes this perfect picture,—so perfect, too, that each season brings its own special beauty to the view. Back from the water a little distance, on higher ground, may be seen the comfortable houses of the farmers. Without indicating the presence of great wealth, the whole appearance of the region is one of thrift and abundance. There is no sign of the "take-it-as-it-comes" spirit which is so common south of Annapolis; the air of the place rather speaks, "Make the most of it." Turkey Point, high and timber-clad, the location of an important lighthouse, stands like a sentinel between the Elk and the wide, shoal mouth of the Susquehanna River.

Probably one should say as little in harsh character about wind or weather as possible when cruising, for he can alter neither one nor the other; neither does it indicate a well-ordered mind to find fault with that which cannot be helped, and which, even if we could alter, would probably be the worse for the interference. Still, as a simple inquiry, it may be allowed us to ask,—how many days of the summer season does the southern-bound navigator find head-winds to contend with on the upper, or indeed the whole, Chesapeake Bay?

By four in the afternoon we entered what is known to fisher-men, oystermen, and others of aquatic tastes as Still Pond Harbor. It lies just south of where the Sassafras River empties, or rather opens, into the Chesapeake. That which is taken for the harbor generally is but a deep indentation or bay opening to the west, and hence, with a wind from the same direction, is merely a trap from which there can hardly be an escape, and in which one must ride out a sea backed by the width of the bay. In the October gale, some years ago, there were several "oyster-pungies" lost in this

fields grow unhedged to the water. It was from within these low uplands that we caught our first glimpse of lightning bugs, or fireflies. I remember that, as a child, chasing after fireflies was one of the wonders of the summer season. A friend who spent a summer in Japan told us about a firefly festival that takes place there in midsummer. Thousands of fireflies are imported to a garden where viewers dine, drink sake, and compose verse to describe the beauty and their delight in the spectacle. Fireflies only have wings with which to fly during the last week or so of their life cycle and during these important days they devote themselves to propagation, blinking their invitations to courtship. I felt a little ashamed to think that I chased and captured these insects as a child, filling a glass jar, fascinated by the sparkling lights. As I watched the fireflies here in Still Pond now as an adult, I knew one

Still Pond

35

The crew of the "Martha"

very harbor; so, at least, I was informed. I had good reason for knowing that there was one such unfortunate there as late as 1879, for, entering the harbor about dark in the evening with the schooner "Alice M," we fairly struck upon the wreck,—fortunately for us, however, with no evil results. Not a sign marked the presence of this dangerous obstacle save the "wake" or ripple made by the wreck itself.

The Still Pond is an offshoot or an inland prolongation of the harbor, and with which it is connected by an inlet say seventy feet wide and twice or thrice as long. That we found it and came to anchor in it, as but few yachtsmen do, I am indebted entirely to the sagacity and the pluck of "Lew," to whom, by the way, I have not yet introduced the reader.

"Lew" is a comely, open-hearted yachtsman, of say twenty-one, whom I was fortunate enough to secure as assistant before I left the Delaware. He is experienced, companionable, and trust-

The crew of the *Response*

didn't have to be a nature lover to feel romantic about them. Perhaps it is this kind of experience that sailing the Bay encapsulates for us. In one single day, we can experience the fluid motion and breezy exhilaration of the sail, then settle down to an evening that is quiet and pure in its singular beauty.

Moses had slept all the way, a fact which I first attributed to her seaworthiness. Maybe it was seasickness, considering how quiet she was during those first days of sailing compared to the rest of the journey. Since I have not talked about her before, I introduce her now to the reader.

Moses was a twelve-week-old kitten we brought along on this cruise in the spirit of recapitulating great-grandfather's experience. Because we had neither need nor room for a bona fide crew member to assist us in our sailing, I came upon the idea of the kitten. During the course of his 1883 cruise, great-grandfather

37

worthy; and I can only hope that in future I may never meet with a worse or less man that Lewis Seaman. It was through him, as I have said, that we found the way into Still Pond. I had been in the harbor before, and had not found the pond. He had not been there before, but did find it. That is just the difference. He noticed the inlet and saw how rapidly the tide ran out, and at once reasoned there must be a large body of water behind the inlet to force a current through with such velocity.

So we headed for the inlet, and gradually saw how it increased in size as we approached, until, when in its mouth, the pond opened to our view; but the current, which suggested the pond, well-nigh prevented our reaching it. The wind died away as we approached the inlet, and when we were in it, ceased entirely. So the anchor was dropped, and then "Lew,"taking a rope over his shoulder, went ashore. I hoisted the anchor on board, and "Lew" towed the yacht through into the mouth of the pond. East and west the land-locked, beautiful pond spread out before us. Every one who is fond of water has some ideal harbor which suggests perfect safety, easy landing on attractive shores, and what more each must add for himself to complete the picture. To me, when longing for a week on the water, this one, Still Pond, is ever uppermost in my mind. I often plan a whole vacation spent there. There is room enough for a large fleet in the pond, but, unfortunately, the bar across the mouth prevents vessels drawing more than three feet of water from entering. My chart shows on the southern shore of this harbor another arm, much like this on the north, but I have never explored it. In the interest of humanity, it is to be hoped that means may be taken to deepen the channel into this Still Pond; for it is doubly hard that men should perish, as in that October gale, when there is an absolutely secure anchorage in full sight.

Considered from another stand-point, this place is one of those glorious surprises which so often strike a person cruising in the Chesapeake. Not only did the beauty of the spot take possession of me as soon as it was disclosed, but within half an hour after we had

had two assistants in the sail—first Lew, then Moses. I persuaded Joe that a kitten named Moses on board would add to the authenticity we were attempting to capture in replicating great-grandfather's trip. We were already acquainted with the pleasures of having a cat for a pet, having two such creatures at home. Cats are readily adaptable to sailing; there is no worry about dinghying them to shore for a walk or to answer nature's call. Caught in a moment of weakness, Joe agreed that a kitten could become part of the crew. Surprisingly, our problem was in obtaining one. At other times of the year, there are notices on bulletin boards with the offer of a kitten "free to a good home". The kitten is often described as litter trained, which is amusing since that is more a feature of the species than an individual achievement. Nevertheless, when once we decided we wanted a kitten, none could be found, litter trained or otherwise. Finally, chance conversation at the hairdresser's brought instant results. One of the hairdressing staff had a litter and said we could have a kitten of our choice. After much discussion about the color and sex, Donald Humphries picked out one for us, raising her from the litter, dubbed as "Mose," which became her nickname.

Mose became a celebrity in her own right at the salon. That she was intended to become a crew member on a historic retracing of a Chesapeake cruise enchanted everyone. On the predetermined day, she was delivered in a wicker basket, a scented ball of silver grey whose green eyes looked with astonishment at the circle of people who had come to bid her bon voyage.

Our veterinarian suggested that we make her a personal flotation device out of styrofoam cups, and offered more mundane advice about treating any on board ailments. Having received the requisite inoculations, and being pronounced fit for the cruise, Mose officially became a crew member. She was totally unperturbed by weather pronouncements or wind conditions, always finding pleasure and fun in her surroundings.

We made our way to Worton Creek on a bright and sunny morning, quite satisfied that today's leg was a short one. As we

39

dropped anchor, Lew's net had caught all the fish we needed for supper. Had the Pilgrim Fathers landed here instead of where they did, it is doubtful whether their piety and importance would have allowed them to stop short of the belief that a spot so delightful and so prolific was created specially for them, and the work of Indian extermination might have been prosecuted with intense zeal. Pike, yellow neds, perch, catfish! Surely such a bill of fare might well awaken the enthusiasm of any man with a yachts-man's appetite, even if he were absolutely devoid of his sporting proclivities.

Every hour of day or night appeared to me to have brought some peculiar sound. In the morning we had catbirds, blackbirds, kingfishers, and fish-hawks; at noon, a family of crows, young and old, kept up a most persistent and vigorous cawing. Whether the last was a lesson in elocution for the junior members of the family I cannot say, though there appeared to be some object and some method in it. At night a legion of frogs gave us a prolonged high-toned serenade.

Close along the northern shore there is a clean, gravelly bottom, and a somewhat greater depth of water than a little farther out, where, on top of the gravel, a slimy, dark, oozy mud is deposited. The tide at that point appeared to flow more rapidly along-shore. Examining the mud microscopically, we found much decaying, loamy matter, some very fine sand, and a number of the silicious skeletons of diatoms. I never saw so many, or such industrious fish-hawks. All day long we could hear them coming down with a splash into the water. Of course an occasional bald eagle appeared, to exact his contribution from the hawks. Even the crows seem to be unusually aquatic in their habits here. I saw one go down into the water almost as recklessly as the fish-hawks did. High grounds and low grounds were close by our anchorage, and we found the yellow clover, the small verbena, the blue-flag, and the mountain-laurel all within a stone's throw of where we lay.

This was not the first time I have wondered why men will sail without a barometer on board. We had a fine thunder-storm, and from our point of safety could enjoy it. The heavy thunder and

40

found our way in, we were again well pleased that we had been resolute in our insistence on a shallow draft boat. That determination had narrowed the field of selection, but our eventual purchase of the *Response* had never left us sorry. We moved easily over the shoal waters into the creek, deciding to anchor out rather than find a slip at the Worton Creek Marina. This marina offers all of the amenities that the modern sailor demands, but whether that would have pleased great-grandfather, I rather doubt. Nonetheless, the progress of the last hundred years has deemed that good facilities and good anchorages are sometimes synonymous. We were in the creek early enough to find an anchorage among the many sailboats moored there. The fact that it was summer and a weekday rather than the weekend gave us the opportunity to enjoy Worton at its best—quiet and uncrowded. Among the sailboats awaiting their weekend occupants flew a multitude of blue heron. The great number of them also perched in the trees surrounding the harbor surprised us. We discovered that nearby Pooles Island is a rookery; these herons had found their way to Worton, and we enjoyed their company.

The trip to Annapolis gave us time to study and practice the fine art of spinnaker sailing. To the novice, going the same way that the wind is going appears to be the easy, ideal way to go. Before I knew much about boats or boating, it seemed to me that the simplest thing to do was to cast off in the same direction as the wind, and just go. Sailing against the wind seemed not only impossible but foolish. Who would want to work so hard at something that is supposed to be so pleasurable? Couple that simplistic notion with the spectacle of spinnaker sailing, the wind blowing on and filling out the colorful striped curves of the sail, and one could easily think that it was aesthetically and functionally the ideal way.

Accomplished sailors, however, value the variety of experience sailing brings. For my spouse, who shouts the orders from the helm, it is often called a challenge. Nevertheless, it didn't start out as much of a challenge on this June day. The gentle breeze into which we hoisted the spinnaker was a puff of friendly

vivid lightning and puffy squalls would have combined with the rain, which came down in force, to make sailing in the bay unpleasant enough. When we had anchored, there was not a cloud in sight; but for all this the barometer warned us to prepare. We did so. There is always more or less danger in sailing the bays in small craft, and it is simply common sense to take the lesser risk which the barometer affords.

Monday, the 11th, we were off by six in the morning. It was natural that we should leave Still Pond with regret. We had no reason to anticipate finding other harbors both as safe and as pleasant. Let me say to other yachtsmen that, in going out the inlet, back-flows and baffling winds may very often, if not usually, be expected as the bluff, where the pond narrows into the inlet, is passed. Sometimes these uncertain elements cause no little trouble in "working ship" where the channel is so narrow.

Once out in the bay the little "Martha" encountered the full force of a strong head-wind, and fairly danced on the waves like a cork. White-caps were forming on all sides. The wind was puffy and uncertain,—now almost a calm, when the boat would lose her headway and lie like a log; then in an instant a violent puff would strike the sail, knocking the yacht down, rail to the water, before she could gather speed enough to make her mind the helm. We now appreciated the full value of the fixed iron ballast. More would have been better, as the excessive buoyancy was a disadvantage in these short, choppy seas. Ballasted, as the boat had been the previous year, with sand, most of which was hardly below the water-line, such sailing must have been dangerous in the extreme. The amazing stupidity of many yacht-owners is absolutely a marvel. Most of those with whom I spoke before placing the iron in my vessel were rather inclined to tender their sympathy that I could be stupid enough to buy iron when I could pick up sand or stones. The reason why I did not buy more and place it where it belonged, outside in the form of an iron keel, was because it involved an expense greater than I felt at liberty to incur. The worst fault was not lack of stiffness, but great buoy-

air. It seemed that we were traveling more slowly than we were, which is a natural impression when going before the wind. At this leisurely pace we made our way towards Annapolis, lulled by the serenity of azure skies reflected on the shimmering waters, with our wake telling us how well we were making way. We played a bit with the sails, trimming them one way, checking our knotmeter for an efficiency rating, then changing things about, and comparing our speed. As I duly recorded all of the readings in our log, I began to muse that we should have named our boat *My Sanity* or some similar name that would more accurately describe the peace of mind we obtained from being on her. Far away from the pressures and chores of our workaday worlds, we could experience life with a calm and untroubled outlook, and the spirit of comradeship which characterizes our marriage was certainly enhanced. Joe is the expert sailor. I like to try my hand, but when push comes to shove, I'd rather do as I am directed to do.

As we drew near to Sandy Point, the wind, which had changed direction, also changed force. More hearty now, it seemed to reach into the spinnaker and give it a good shake; the spinnaker lifted itself up, pulling us hard, then lost the burst it had captured and began to flop and shake in the aftermath. The main would then try to adjust itself, swinging out into the wind until the lines were taut and creaking from its effort. I took the helm as Joe clambered around on deck, adjusting lines and checking tackles. As he pulled on the spinnaker sheet, the sails whipped out again with the wind, and the boat began to roll. Holding firm on the tiller, I began to feverishly review in my mind the man overboard routine, for I envisioned Joe being knocked right off the deck by the force of a line or the roll of the boat. I didn't like what he was doing on deck one bit, but I had learned to master my fear and my tongue, and trust to his judgment and expertise. We never did, of course, come close to a rollover, but it felt to me as if we were, which only goes to show that feelings aren't facts!

The remainder of the crossing from eastern to western shore was made under main and jib, the spinnaker having been duly bagged and stowed for another day's cruising. With calmness

ancy. Lew remarked, in a quiet way, "This boat takes the trouble to go right over the tops of all these waves." So it was; for sometimes she actually appeared to jump half her length out of the water.

Three miles ahead we sighted another point, one which marked a tempting harbor. The tide had turned and was against us; this, with the adverse winds and waves, decided us to put into the harbor,—Worton's Creek. The attempt to beat down to Annapolis involved a long, hard day's work, with no pleasure whatever in the sail. Giving the yacht more sheet, we headed for the creek, entering it in good style, flying past a party of fishermen who were running out an immensely long seine. Once fairly in, we sighted two arms, one of which ran northward, opening into a considerable expanse of water, the other and more inviting one extending toward the south. We beat into the latter about a mile, and dropped our anchor opposite to Buck Neck Landing. Shortly afterward the steamer "Van Corlear," from Baltimore, came in and afforded us a chance to send off our mail.

For a while the place appeared to be alive, carriages thronging the wharves to receive those coming, and to help away those who were leaving. But they departed with the steamer, and in half an hour the place resumed its wonted quietness. Dreaminess appeared to rule the hours. For the rest of the day hardly a sign of life was visible. I made several attempts to purchase some rope which I needed on the yacht, but found the merchant was taking a nap, or had gone visiting, or was somewhere else than in his store. Late in the evening the desired purchase was made. The law of compensation, it is evident, runs through the whole of the universe outside of ourselves. I am convinced now that it at last decides the individual destiny. Were it not for some such law, men at Buck Neck Landing might live forever, or certainly as long as the patriarchs. The world's troubles do not appear to concern them, the world's thoughts never agitate them; come peace, come war, nerve-tissues and myosin are renewed as fast as expended, and but for some beneficent disease or accident men would never leave there to stay even in Paradise. The place would be over-

restored to my heart and our progress, we reviewed our troubles with the spinnaker and analyzed our actions and reactions. Joe has a favorite maxim for controlling the boat and the boater's actions, which goes, "you may scramble, but never hurry!" Scrambling, in his mind, is deliberate speed; hurrying is likely to be careless, leading to less desirable outcomes.

On this day in early June there were few other boats on the water. In the fall of the year, however, Sandy Point is the location of a wonderful celebration called Chesapeake Appreciation Days. During the weekend of Appreciation Days, workboats—skipjacks, and other "traditional" Bay boats—crowd the waters and thrill the spectator with their recollections of the Chesapeake's past. Being berthed in St. Michaels, we have a rich and ready opportunity to view the historical traditions of the Bay during the summer months, when we are devoted weekend residents. Up the Bay, or in the Chester River across from Sandy Point, one of our real pleasures is watching the log canoe races. Log canoes, of course, were not designed originally for racing or for pleasure; they are the antecedents of the Chesapeake Bay dead rise workboat used by many watermen today. The Indians introduced Bay settlers to their boat-building methods; with ingenuity, they burnt and dug out logs to use in fishing the waters on which they lived. A log was aptly suited to the navigation of the shallow waters of the Bay. What began as a single-logged vessel grew into one constructed out of three to five logs, enlarged to accommodate the bounty of oysters, crabs, and fish culled from the Chesapeake.

At the turn of the twentieth century, when log canoes had just about reached the peak of their career as working vessels, ten to fifteen million bushels of oysters were being harvested each year. The broad-beamed, shallow draft log canoe was sound and sturdy, perfectly suited to the oysterman's need for a vessel that could meet the challenge of shallow waters and still accommodate the catch. The demise of the log canoe as a workboat was not due to its lack of seaworthiness, but probably more a direct result of the simple unavailability of trees large enough to hew into canoes.

45

crowded. With fish in the waters and fruit on the land, these kind-hearted, generous, and honest inhabitants would remain, in quiet and in sunshine, until they multiplied enough to wear their clothing out by jostling against each other.

There was a solitary living exception to what I have said, visible from meridian until four P.M. A good-natured colored boy amused himself by the hour sculling a heavy "yawl-boat" over to the western side of the creek; then, hoisting a broad board in the bow for a sail, he threw himself down in the stern of the boat and scudded before the wind back to the eastern shore. He was full of the languid poetry of drifting; his whole soul was saturated with it, though it never found expression. The solitary reader of his Muse was myself. Happiness is a purely relative term. This, of course, is a platitude. But who of all mankind ever come to fully appreciate the breadth of even so plain a thing, and to rest content with the present? I have in mind now two who illustrate the extremes. One of them is that young negro. He came alongside, and I gave him a bucket of preserved prunes, which neither Lew nor myself could tolerate. He received them with open eyes and mouth. If he only knew how little generosity there was in that gift, we would suffer in his estimate. He soon became to full of happiness on preserved prunes even to enjoy the pleasure of crossing the creek behind his board-sail. We saw him on the other side, with his feet hanging over the boat and receiving the caress of the water, just as his face, upturned to the sun, was comforted by the superheated rays. An hour later Pompey came alongside again. For the gift of a cigar he consented to have his "picture tuk,"

Marked on the lower part of the store building I found the statement, "High-water mark. September 17, 1876." It was gratifying to obtain the fact, not only because it was a fact and indicated a storm-tide several feet higher than common, but because it evinced interest in an unusual event. However, two months later I should have seen busy times on that very quiet wharf, when the peach crop, one great interest of the region, was being shipped. We went ashore during the evening, and enjoyed the hospitality

Couple the exploitation of nature's bounty (which would have been substance for great-grandfather's rallying and railing) with the advent of the motor as an accessory to sail, and it is easy to understand the evolution of the deadrise workboat. Possessing the attributes of the log canoe in its ability to move through the water with ease, the workboat of today is frame built, with a storage house installed forward where the mast used to be. Steady and sturdy, these workboats are time-tested craft that are synonymous with recollections from the past.

The log canoe, passing from an oyster-tonging model that was built up and down the Eastern Shore, can be seen today as a racing craft that competes throughout the summer months in races held around the Bay. The canoes are owned privately, and crewed by loyal, nimble men and women who devote a good deal of their leisure time to maintaining and racing the boats. St. Michaels is the home of quite a few of the canoes, and it is not uncommon for a fifty-foot wooden mast to be lying on the dock in front of the *Response*'s slip at Higgins Yacht Yard, waiting for four or five of the crew to step it and walk it upright. Our loyalty is to the one owned by our yacht yard friends, the *Island Lark*. Tad and Ebbie duPont own the *Lark*, and Joe has spent many years as their erstwhile follower and tagalong. I often kid him about going out to play with his friends at the boat yard, and one of his favorite times to be with these friends is when the *Lark* is in home port. There is fascination and delight in getting her ready, even when that means only lending an occasional hand to the crew that maintains and races her.

Some of the same yard crew who work on our boat work on and crew the *Lark*, so we see them and know them better than any of the other St. Michaels residents. From our observation point, it was evident that log canoe racing is work as much as it is pleasure, and that work extends itself from the care of the boat to the sailing of it. With the motor of our boat idling and our binoculars fixed, we often followed the *Lark*'s races, cheering our favorite's progress. It is true that, from late April until late October, we are

Sandy Point Lighthouse

and conversation of one of the near residents.

Tuesday, the 12th, we left our anchorage on the last of the ebb tide, and headed south for Annapolis. We hoped by making an early start to reach our destination in spite of the adverse and heavy weather. So we did, but it was at the cost of vast patience and severe buffeting. As the crow flies, the distance would have been considerably less than thirty miles. In a fair wind the run would have been a very short one; but in a small boat, with wind and tide both against us, it consumed a great part of the day. Yet it appeared that we were not much worse off than others who were in sight and bound the same way. Harbor after harbor was passed, until by 2 P.M. it was clear that, even with the odds against us, reaching our destination was merely a question of time and perse-

Sandy Point Lighthouse

loathe to make any engagements that keep us at home on the weekends; that is especially true on race weekends, which we mark on the calendar as soon as we get the schedule. The Miles River Yacht Club, of which we are members, is the "home of the log canoes," and Perry Cabin, which is around the corner, hosts a log canoe racing weekend each year which is one of our favorites; we are, so to speak, surrounded by the work and excitement of the races and would need to be nearly senseless not to be caught up in it. We remain on the periphery, impressed by the rigorous dedication of the racers (and their families, who give them up most weekends with great good spirit), and involved inextricably with the romance and nostalgia of these beautiful boats, sleekly and slimly rising up and sailing out of the past.

verance. Hoping to avoid the force of the waves, we left the eastern shore and started for the other side. To my surprise, where I expected to find a sheltered shore, the water was almost or quite as rough as the one we had left. The difference in color between the deep-green water and the yellowish hue in shoaler places was strikingly apparent. From Bodkin Point, down along the western shore, the beat appeared almost interminable. We had fully decided at one time on anchoring in Magotha [sic] Harbor. On maturer reflection we both concluded it would be just a little unmanly to remain there over-night, when a friend and prospective shipmate was waiting for us in Annapolis. It did appear, though, as if we never could get by Sandy Point. "It shoals" a long, long way out. Then, too, fellow-yachtsmen, be advised: do not attempt, as we did, to go inside of the buoys off Greenbury Light when it is blowing a gale, unless you know the ground too well to make a mistake. The "Martha" tried the experiment, and, though she did drag over, there was nothing at all to spare. It is very trying to keep outside, especially when the wind is against you, but probably you will find it best to do so.

We received a lesson in naval architecture when crossing from the eastern to the western shore. My boat, being the usual model of the Delaware Bay,—broad and short,—was at her very worst in the head-wind and "choppy sea" of the Chesapeake. She labored severely, with lee rail under (for we were carrying whole sail, though the wind whistled through the rigging), or rose over the waves until it appeared as if more than half the hull was out of water. Alongside us came a Chesapeake "bug-eye,"* of light draught, but long and narrow. We saw her start from Tolchester Beach, and creep up on us swiftly and surely. We were laboring; she was moving along without effort, going not only faster, but working more to the windward. At the very time this forty-foot bug-eye was leaving us, we ourselves were distancing a large coasting schooner. The bug-eye careened over very little, went

*The term "bug-eye" appears to be a corruption of "buck-eye," which name was at first given from the auger-holes on either side of the bow, and through which the cable ran.

The log canoes are not the only testimonial to Bay history offered by St. Michaels. Indeed, the Chesapeake Bay Maritime Museum is dedicated to marking the maritime progress of the Bay, and in its nineteen-year history has grown to gain national recognition. One of the highlights of the Member's Day Weekend activities is the racing of the museum's traditional boats. Among these is a log-bottomed bugeye, *Edna E. Lockwood,* as well as a skipjack and a schooner complete with gaff topsail. I often think of this museum in terms of adjectives rather than nouns, which is perhaps a reflection of how it impresses me rather than a disparagement of its fine collection. It is charming, and we visit it frequently, both as members and as hosts to our weekend guests. It is quite educationally oriented, and I think it would be fair to claim that as its emphasis. It offers a number of courses for which Joe and I yearn to have the time; when we talk of our retirement, there is room for attendance at some of the programs, especially in estuarine studies, as we desire to become more knowledgeable and responsible in using the Bay.

We did not make the ninety-mile run to Smith Creek in one day. Knowing that we would be able to catch up later in the cruise, since we didn't plan to sail backwards as great-grandfather had had to do once or twice, we headed instead for Solomons. With a five-knot southwesterly wind, we headed down bay with main and jib splayed against the early morning haze. The breeze kicked up later in the morning, and some white caps danced on the water to remind us that the going was good. With a fair amount of heel, we made six knots around Drum Point, carefully dodging fish nets, a feat we were to repeat over and over again on this southern leg. Mose paid no attention to our "watch to starboard" shouts, sleeping on the cabin floor when our heel made a perch on a cushion seat untenable. By two-thirty we were just coming up on the Solomons Island Yacht Club when two low flying jets pierced the sky with a terrific roar, tearing aside all sound except their own echo. Mose, who had only just joined us on deck, not yet liking sailing enough to be out when the going was rough, abandoned us

easily through the water, made no pounding or splashing, and looked almost into the wind. Thus she proved herself as possessing every requisite of a first-class sea-goer. It is doubtful if she drew more than two feet and a half of water; it is much more probable that she drew less. She certainly did not have ballast enough to sink her if she had filled with water. These were all most desirable features in a small boat. But here was a direct violation of what we have been taught were cardinal features in small-boat construction,—shallowness and small beam on the one hand, and great length, with no ballast, and shallowness on the other. The present ruling fashion is that a small boat shall be at least four times as long as broad, and that she shall carry, say, half her tonnage, or more, deep down in the water, in the shape of a lead or iron keel. It is certain that a boat built after this, the English cutter model, may "knock down"; but it is certain she will not stay down. Unless she fills, she must right again. I believe that, so far as our American sloop and the English cutter have come into fair trial, the cutter has proven the better boat,—safer and faster. I am not sure what the result of a contest between the cutter and the bug-eye would be. From what I have seen of the latter class of boats in the Chesapeake, I am most strongly prepossessed in their favor. The model of this nondescript is peculiar. Probably the light cedar gunning-skiff which does duty as a yawl-boat for us is as nearly an exact imitation of the bug-eye model as one can imagine. Now, that same skiff, with sharp bow and stern, such as the bug-eye was, gave us, when we towed it down to Annapolis through heavy seas, a most astonishing illustration of sea-worthiness. Every vessel we met had her yawl swung up, or on deck. Yet our yawl rode so easily that the line by which we towed her was seldom stretched, and not a tin-cupful of water worked into her during the whole day. The best statement I can give of the bug-eye model is one furnished to *Forest and Stream* by "Talbot." Here it is. The accompanying illustration will give a general idea of the appearance of the craft. It should be added, however, that the smaller vessels of this class have all their sails triangular in shape.

with the kind of speed that accompanies terror. I rather doubt that she had ever heard anything as loud as these jets, and cared nothing for watching their majestic silhouettes as they banked and turned in perfect symmetry. I found them fascinating and breath-taking, watching them with childish delight. Eyes drawn, I felt unrestrained exuberance at their fly-by, still smiling at the sight as we came into the yacht club.

It has been our desire, like great-grandfather, to see some-thing of the places we visit. Securing the *Response*, we ambled "into town," strolling around in the afternoon sun. There is a maritime museum, and stores and restaurants easily reached from the water. By the time we got back on board, we were ready for showers and cool drinks. Books in hand, we spent the evening reading, a pleasure that we share.

We departed the Solomons Island Yacht Club at the leisurely hour of 10 A.M., photographing the abandoned lighthouse at Cedar Point on our way out of the Patuxent. Joe's mother had loved lighthouses, and had painted us a set of place mats with ones situated along the New England coast. We had gotten in the habit of shooting Bay lighthouses for her collection, and even though our original inspiration was no longer with us, we had grown accustomed to seeking out these bastions of stone for their artistic interest. With a following sea, we hoisted the spinnaker and enjoyed a smooth sail. Mose, lured out on deck by our tuna fish lunch, stayed to enjoy the sun and breeze. In the early afternoon we fixed the jib with a whisker pole, and averaged a slow but consistent three-and-and-a-half knots under wing and wing. At four-thirty our anchor was down in Smith Creek, where we had none but a lone workboat for company.

Shortly after our arrival, the workboat departed, and in sol-itude we enjoyed the lovely and quiet surroundings. Great clumps of yellow honeysuckle covered some of the tree trunks, making a splashy spot of color. Fir trees loaded with cones dotted the cove. A few of the trees grew at a remarkable angle to the water; whether from soil erosion or sunseeking, they looked al-most as if they had been fixed there by a modernist who had

CHESAPEAKE BUG-EYES

Editor *Forest and Stream:*

The inquiry contained in your paper concerning the bug-eye, as it is called by our oystermen, is a step in the right direction, and Mr. Roosevelt can obtain any information he may desire from Captain James L. Harrison, Tilghman's Island P.O., Talbot County, Maryland. Captain Harrison is the builder of the fastest boat of this type on the Chesapeake. If this model is peculiar to our section, there remains in store a treat for all who adopt it in other waters, where speed and safety are desired. The boat is not perfectly flat-bottomed, as Mr. Roosevelt supposes, but built so as to combine light draught and carrying capacity. The centre-board is constant, also single head-gear. The jigger is always stepped so as to trim the sheets to traveller on deck. Many of them are built with round sterns with overhang, as in the cutter. Schooner rig prevails to great extent, but adds nothing to speed. These boats are extremely fast, and brave the heaviest gales of our winter. Larger vessels often capsize, but the bug-eye never. I enclose you the dimensions of the boat thought to be the fastest in the whole fleet, with a sketch showing rig: length, fifty feet; beam, twelve and one-half feet; dead rise, one and one-half inches to the foot; draught, light, three feet; centreboard, twelve feet.

Talbot

It appears from the above, especially when one remembers the sharp-sterned "pinkies" of half a century ago on the New England coast, and which were so remarkable for sea-going qualities, that in estimating all the good lines in a boat-model we must probably give considerable importance to the shape of the stern. Indeed, some assert that the shape of the latter is of as much importance as that of the bow. I have a half-conviction that, taken all in all, these same bug-eyes are as fast and as safe as many of our renowned yachts of the same size.

The evolution or mode of development of the bug-eye is interesting. So far as now appears, the whole fleet of them grew out of the equally famous Chesapeake log canoe,—"Kunners," as the negroes and some of the illiterate whites called them. These originally were made from three large pine logs, which were

Abandoned lighthouse on Patuxent River

undertaken to sculpt the surroundings. On the beach of the cove reposed some nice pieces of driftwood. A large black crow busily stalked the beach, while other birds sang little short melodies to each other from the trees. I have never quite agreed with the person who classified crows as songbirds, but as this one did not join in the refrain, it caused no reason for complaint. By six-thirty a light rain had begun, and we withdrew into the cabin. It was a quiet, cool ending to a warm, sunny day. As we settled into our bunks, the soft rain tattooed a faint memory of the past onto the cabin roof.

We were awakened in the morning by the discordant chattering of birds and the strong light of yet another fine day. Rousing ourselves, we pulled anchor in waters unbroken by even a faint ripple of air, and started out. As we made our way slowly out of the creek,

55

neatly and strongly jointed together by three dressed faces, so that one made the bottom and the other two the sides. These were hollowed out and finely shaped outside. Being nothing but wood, they were of course unsinkable, besides being extremely strong, tight, and durable. Then two long masts, which had a most wonderful rake, were added. A jib was, or was not, reckoned part of the outfit. These Chesapeake canoes did their work so well that they became the popular small boat of the region, and to increase their size and carrying capacity the largest available logs were used. Still, the limit in size did not appear to have been reached, and the model is essentially preserved in boats now framed and planked up in the ordinary ship style. These are the latest product of Chesapeake naval genius, and are the popular bug-eyes. The small modifications of the canoe type which they have introduced are somewhat more "dead rise" and more swell amidships. It may be well for our yacht constructors, before absolutely and finally adopting the deep English type as the most suitable vessel for our waters, to examine very carefully into the claims of these non-descripts. Chesapeake naval-constructive genius cannot well be despised. It has too famous a place in the history of the Baltimore clipper, which a generation ago so astonished the world. To my mind the secret of their wonderful stiffness remains unsolved. Oystermen say they will live out a storm longer than any other model on the bay. There is no other style growing more in favor with these men than the bug-eye. Hence, then, a fair trial, if for no other reason than to test the value of an American type.

A day could not be spared, on our way down, to see the points of interest in and about Annapolis without a serious break in our plans. However, as we found a friend (Lieutenant Bull, of the navy), the break was made, and the time spent in the grounds of the Naval Academy, under his guidance, was a more than sufficient compensation for waiting.

When we left, on the morning of the 14th, we were comforted by the assurance, received the day before, that we might expect head-winds going down the bay about nine days out of ten at that season. However, thanks to the squall of the previous evening,

I saw a fin approaching to port, and very excitedly pronounced that there was an enormous fish heading for the boat. As it came close, I was able to see that it was a large ray, whose surface was just visible under the water before it took a splashy dive under the hull. It gave the illusion of being very large, swimming there just under the water, and it appeared quite ominous, not at all the kind of thing which enticed one to get another look. It was the first of many rays we were to encounter on the trip, and we finally grew rather used to their presence.

Rounding Smith Point, we found ourselves in Virginia waters. The morning calm remained with us, despite an earlier weather report that had predicted winds up to twenty knots. Since those wind predictions turned out to be considerably exaggerated, we continued for a good while under motor. Later, we hoisted the jib for the fun of it, and picked up half a knot, which did indicate that there was some air going. Now a motor sailer, we continued uneventfully on our way, with no cause throughout our thirty-six-mile journey to test the skill of the skipper or crew.

Arriving in Milford Haven, we thought we would go through to the other side of the bridge and find an anchorage. A bit off the bridge, we gave the customary long and a short on the horn, without any results on the part of the bridgetender. Circling around, we peered at the bridge house through binoculars and tried the horn again. As there was still no response, we made our way to the Narrows Marina and Islander Motel, thinking we would pick up some fuel and solve the mystery of getting the swing bridge to swing. While so doing, we met a young man about twelve, who leaned against his bike and chatted with us for a bit about the marina. After he had told us about the pool, and the restaurant, and the car that would take us to the grocery shop, we decided to abandon anchoring out in favor of the facilities of the Narrows. We laughingly told our young bicycling acquaintance that he had convinced us to stay, suggesting that the marina might use someone with his sales ability on the payroll. With that, he proudly and unabashedly told us that his Dad owned the marina, assured us that we would enjoy our dinner, and departed with a

the wind had hauled around to the north, and we had a fresh breeze following us all day. So that, after a run of ninety miles, we dropped our anchor for the night in Smith's Creek, a little offshoot from the Potomac. The small number of sails we saw in making the run was a surprise, bearing no comparison to what we expected, or to what we should certainly have seen had we been on the Delaware. Still, it is hard to think that Baltimore, with its superb water-approaches, will long lag in the race.

The little bay, for such it was, in which we had anchored was completely landlocked, and not more than two hundred yards wide; yet it contained water enough for a good-sized vessel. This abundance of superior harbors may be considered as a peculiarity in which the Chesapeake is pre-eminent. This, along with the navigable waters, estuaries, and rivers intersecting the land in all directions, has in one sense retarded the development of the country,—i.e., by making water communication so easy and so extensive, it has in so far superseded the necessity for roads. The sailing canoe is the ordinary means of travel from place to place along the shores. This retarding effect was observed even by the early colonial writers.

June 15th still gave us, in the morning, a promising northerly wind, and we started out early, hoping to make a big run to the southward that day. It was, however, 4 P.M. when we reached Milford Haven, on the Piankatank River. Our intention had been to push on down to Mob-jack Bay, but the weakening wind warned us to seek a harbor while we could have daylight to do it in. No rule can be regarded as invariable when one's doings depend upon the uncertainties of wind and weather. It was my desire, however, to always be at anchor by three in the afternoon. This allowed a turn on the shore to see what could be found, and gave us a chance to take in all the surroundings, and decide what we would do in any emergency which might arise during the night.

Milford Haven is still another of those surprises which con-

Milford Haven

friendly wave of the hand. We were very entertained by this twist of fate, and not at all sorry afterwards that we had stayed. We learned from the dockmaster that three blasts were the magic number for arousing the bridge keeper, and promptly made note of it. Yet, later in the evening, a Coast Guard buoy tender approached, blew a long and a short, and promptly proceeded through a bridge which opened for it, which makes one wonder if bigger isn't better after all.

The buoy tender was not only bigger, it was louder, which led to some little excitement on Mose's part. While we were sitting on the stern, she was exploring up forward, and made the discovery that the dock was in close proximity to the boat, a mistake we were not to make very often again. The blast of the horn startled her

stantly greet one yachting along the western shore of the Chesapeake. Now, as elsewhere, we were landlocked for the night. The entrance, which at first appeared too small to admit a vessel, widens out into a broad, deep mouth, and inside the harbor which it leads to a whole fleet of canoes and some good-sized schooners lay. During the evening spent there, Mr. J. and Lew occupied themselves catching crabs. Half an hour of the sport was sufficient to cover the deck with vigorous pugnacious specimens, who the night through manifested their excessive vitality by threatening anyone audacious enough to leave the cabin in the dark hours. However, this was more than compensated for when we came to enjoy them cooked. There is a difference in flavor of crabs, just as there is in that of oysters; and for both Milford Haven is justly famous. Cape May "goodies," served up with the oysters and crabs, make one even now, after the lapse of several months, remember our anchorage in the Piankatank with feelings of complete satisfaction.

There was a source of annoyance in our charts. These were all that we could desire out in the deep water, but along-shore, in water where we thought we could go, they gave us no information. The score of little bays and harbors that one "might make," if only his chart would indicate the depth of water or show him the way in, were a constant aggravation, because we knew there were such, and such quiet places, too, as we most desired to enter with camera in hand. Chart-makers, we shoal-water yachtsmen, we owners of very small craft, do beseech you to give the channel and the depth of water into every small harbor in the Chesapeake. Our experience at the mouth of the Potomac was provoking. The chart led us to put in there because of a small safe harbor which was indicated; but we searched in vain for it, and were obliged to make a considerable run out of our way to find a secure anchorage.

June 16th found us astir by sunrise, which this season of the year means by about half-past four. We thought ourselves early risers, but the partridges were up before us, and we could hear their musical whistle from all sides. Is it so that there are early and late risers among our daybirds? It was not until long after the "Bob

into unthinking bravery, and the leap of terror she made took her straight onto the dock. What made me turn in time to see her dashing for land, I do not know, but my alarm was considerable that she would be off and lost in the gathering dusk. Up and after her, we did not have to go far before we encountered her little self, exploring with nose and paw some tantalizing earth smell. Once she knew we were there, she insisted on playing a bit, running a short distance, then crouching with head cocked to view our advance. We caught on to the "let's play chase" theme being enacted, and stopped playing the game, whereupon her interest waned and she was coaxed back to the dock and lifted aboard. Returned from her expedition ashore, with heaving sides and lolling tongue she stretched herself in the cabin to regain bodily coolness. She had survived, with remarkable sangfroid, her first encounter with jumping ship.

At 5 A.M. we were awakened by the wake of workboats heading out, and not too long after decided to follow suit. As we swung slowly around and approached the bridge, we chose once again to try a long and a short, which this time got the bridge open. Slowly and deliberately, we traveled east, through what is called locally the "hole in the wall." Where great-grandfather had had a pilot to direct him through this weaving shortcut, we had Coast Guard buoys and locally planted tree branches as navigational aids. The workboats that had awakened us were busily at their trade, with gulls in loyal attendance. The crab pots hoisted on deck had crabs in them so their early start and our rude awakening were obviously not in vain.

There are probably many fascinations that Bay sailors hold in common, and one which surely no one has immunity from is the fascination commanded by the osprey. We had seen quite a few nests in the past day, and again this morning; compared with the ospreys up Bay, these did not chee at us in as much alarm as we moved by their nest. As we were wondering whether this was an extension of southern hospitality, a nearby bird gave its shrill cry and lifted from its nest. Flying overhead, with an easy five-foot wingspan, it looked with eyes six times as powerful as man's for the

White" whistle was heard that the crows began to make themselves conspicuously noisy.

Our anchorage in Milford Haven was on the southern side. The anchor was let go in two fathoms of water, but during the night, swinging with the tide, the yacht had been left stern aground. This accident caused but little delay. We were soon floating, and in less than the length of the yacht were again in the channel, with water enough for a large schooner. Most of these harbors have certain features in common. Thus there is ordinarily a bar at the outlet, where the current of the main body of water, meeting with that coming from the harbor, causes enough retardation of the water to allow the suspended mineral matters to fall to the bottom. Such, at least, is the explanation which forces itself on my mind. There may be a much better one, however, for aught that I know. Then, again, leading to and from all these harbors, there is a strong current where the inlet or outlet is narrow and the harbor is wide. Hence through this narrow part there must be a rapid current, with great capacity for deepening and eroding the channel. This, in fact, is just what we find, and when by storm or otherwise the channel is closed, this swift current very speedily opens another.

There is a tortuous, very narrow channel from Milford Haven out to the bay, in which, by sailing east, we hoped to save important time that would have been lost to have gone out from the north as we came in. A very intelligent colored man, one Richard McKnight, undertook to pilot us through this lower passage. We found him a character, who, between serving during war times as a cook for a northern general and as a sailor, had gathered quite a fund of information. The use he made of his knowledge as we drifted slowly out was very entertaining. His observations upon the animal life around us were quite acute. As for the fish-hawks and the eagles, he seemed to have been taken into their secrets. Their sounds and movements were familiar to him, as those of the little boy who accompanied him. Among other things, he told the local tale as to why the eagle exacted a tribute

telltale ripples of its prey. Feeding exclusively on fish, it had immensely powerful legs, with talons that would be hurled forward for the kill. The dive made, reverse talons hold the wriggling fish, while jointed wings, like an elbow, give the extra power needed to pull up out of the water. What adds to the allure of beauty and power is the fact that ospreys mate for life, and when there are young to be hatched, the male carries out a portion of the incubating chores; this has always appealed to my romantic nature and made me ever enchanted with their spectacle.

We departed from great-grandfather's agenda to make a short stop in Norfolk for the Harborfest. It synchronized so well with this, our first trip south, that we felt almost as if it had been planned that way. Getting there, however, was not half the fun; with another following sea, we passed Wolf Trap, doing a nice five knots under sunny albeit cool skies. We began to pick up a lot of boat traffic, as barges could be seen dotting the horizon and trawling menhaden boats reminded us of the commercial fishing industry of the Bay. The wind was out of the east-northeast, and reported on the radio at fifteen to twenty knots, gusting to twenty-five. The waves were running three to four feet, and Joe was taking constant care to prevent an uncontrolled jibe. Before the wind all the way, we rode into Norfolk like surfers, and we were not the least bit unhappy to throw the anchor down in the Elizabeth River. We dinghied to a floating barge, from which we picked up a launch. After some shopping at the Waterside, and some conversation with Carroll Walker, whose collection of old photographs of Norfolk was exhibited, we returned on board to watch a spectacular fireworks display. Squeals of pleasure could be heard as the rockets hissed their way upward, then burst into colored baubles falling all over the sky. Again and again new ones rushed up, and no one could fail to find delight and a lifted heart during this unrestrained entertainment. It was over too soon, dropping and dripping in one last blast of noise and glory; horns blew in terrific thankfulness, then were quiet. We were glad we had come, and would put Harborfest again on our cruising list.

from the hawk. The former was the earlier inhabitant of the region. When the fish-hawk came, he did not know how to make his nest. This the eagle taught him to do, under promise that the hawk should pay him in fish for the instruction. This obligation was disregarded, and the eagle was obliged to take his due by force.

The run of the 16th was a very short one. We anchored for the night behind New Point Comfort. So far as the weather was concerned, we rested well enough, but there was a fish-mill on shore which was most exasperatingly fragrant. It called to mind some passages from "The Tempest,"—

> *Adrian:* The air breathes upon us here most sweetly.
> *Sebastian:* As if it had lungs, and rotten ones.
> *Antonio:* Or, as 'twere perfumed by a fen.

We asked a negro who came along-side to sell oysters, just after we had anchored, who the females were that, in the absence of the men of the crew, saved their sloop from the vengeance of the governor when he was hunting oyster pirates, a few months before. There was a nice little story going the rounds of the newspapers that these Piankatank women, recognizing the emergency, escaped by themselves getting the anchor and sails up and navigating the vessel to a place of safety. One of our popular illustrated journals gave a page or two of rhyming history of the affair. The negro knew nothing of it; but, if it "was so, he guessed they must have come from the other side." Whether true or not, it illustrates that home praises are often very faint, and that it is only when echoed back from a distance that they are heard at all. Alas for fame!

The United States boat "Fish-Hawk" lay in the same place. We could not just see what she was doing, though, of course, she had some mission there, and was accomplishing it in the usual comfortable, leisurely government way.

Sunday morning, the 17th, the wind was so fair that we concluded to start for Fortress Monroe. An hour before sunrise everything looked unpromising. The wind was not only dead

Instead of making a stop at New Point Comfort or Fortress Monroe, we made our way to Newport News to visit The Mariners Museum. Docking the *Response* at the Warwick Yacht Club, we made our way by hired car to the museum. We had been so full of history on this trip that a museum within boating reach seemed to rivet our attention and mandate our visit. The museum collection was varied and tasteful; it had so much worth comment that for fear of leaving something out, we will only recommend it as a definite addition to every yachter's list of things "to do." Of especial interest to us was the library, to which we were graciously admitted. A little research had revealed to us that we would find Byrd's *Westover Papers* here, which I wanted to review before heading up the James. I spent an enjoyable hour poring over the diaries, resisting the temptation to browse among the other books for time was short and pleasure had to be rationed. We left totally satisfied with our visit, especially after we found that the library boasted an original of great-grandfather's book. I'm sure there are others in personal collections, but we had come all this way before we had encountered one in a library. A museum brochure offered the hope that our visit would enhance our love of the sea—it did.

Leaving the Warwick Yacht Club and the friendly people there, we headed for the James, where the real history buff in us longed to go. Another warm, sunny day, we found ourselves again motoring with our sunshade up. Moving unattended and alone, we passed through the naval reserve fleet, through row after row of anchored cargo ships, all neatly aligned, giving the impression of remarkable, silent strength. With a little imagination, one could liken oneself to a queen reviewing the fleet, such was the sense of omnipotence and pride that accompanied our quiet movement among the ships.

With due care and little water to spare, we found our way to the dock of First Colony, at the upper end of Jamestown Island, where Clyde and Sally Harbison lived. Joe and Clyde had taught a sailing course together one summer, and become a little acquainted, in the way all boaters seem so easily to do. Once we had determined to make this trip, we phoned the Harbison's with the

ahead, but there was too much of it. Any other place was better than where we were. It was certain that we must make a harbor somewhere else. Then, too, the Sabbath in full reach of the odors from a fish-mill! It would have been enough to banish all proper feeling, and to concentrate all one's attention on his nose. So the start was made, and soon, as the old adverse breeze died away, a new and favoring one sprang up. This aided us to the fort by half-past two in the afternoon.

The following day we started up the James, anchoring for the night at the lower end of Jamestown Island. The next evening found us anchored off City Point, where my vacation work was to begin.

The only unpleasant association connected with the place was that my friend, Mr. J., who had been with us for a week, took his departure for the North and the treadmill of life again.

intent of joining up with them for an evening "down south." Like
so many of the people we encountered in the preparation for and
sailing of this cruise, they extended themselves in aiding and
abetting our success. Sally Harbison, whose being a nurse made
us immediate kindred spirits, did much searching out of information for us, having a whole list of resources and phone numbers
ready for us when we met her there on the beach. It was the
people, more than the places, that made our trip so memorable,
and none more than the Harbisons, who were willing to share
their home, car, and dinner table with strange yachting fellows.
Later, in the long winter between the cruise and the writing of
this book, when doubts would assail me, I would remember the
people who had so graciously offered their help, and courage
would return.

CHAPTER III.
DOWN THE JAMES AND UP THE CHESAPEAKE.

TO the next generation City Point will have lost the meaning which it has for thousands of men now living. Its very situation, at the junction of the James and the Appomattox, is full of stirring suggestions. It is strange that the waters which flow past the birthplace of the nation should also have their source so close to the spot where the final struggle for its life and perpetuity was made.

Bermuda Point, City Point, and Petersburg are all associated, geographically and historically, and all were during the recent war a very focus of military operations. Plots and counterplots were worked out there. Troops were embarked and disembarked on the very wharves whose ruins yet remain along-shore. Over those very decaying piles, hundreds, mayhap thousands, of wounded or sick marched, or were carried, on their way to Northern hospitals.

The town itself has but little to speak of. Whatever energy the place indicates is centered along the wharves, where the railroad and the steamboats meet. Rumor says some interest hostile to the growth of the place is at work. It is hard now to picture the sight of troops and engines of war on the very spot which, at the time of our visit, was covered with matured wheat. The only reminder of war that one sees are the six monitors which lie at anchor on the southern side of the channel. One officer, residing in Petersburg, commanded the whole fleet, while a squad of men does duty in allowing the old war-battered vessels to rest and rot in becoming dignity. Their decks are white; the iron, and other things which the unwritten law of the sea demands shall be black, receive their

Chapter 3

OUR first view of City Point made if difficult for us to visualize the sight of troops and war equipment on the shoreline which is now industrialized and hardly reminiscent of any stirring historical events. We journeyed here entirely by motor; the river was hot and airless, and we joked a lot, traveling through such quiet, hazy water, about being on the *African Queen*. Weather conditions like these make photography, as well as pleasure in one's surroundings, difficult; there was a lack of anything very picturesque to photograph without making an entirely negative statement about the area. We did see a number of cormorants perched on islands formed by sunken barges. We were told that these same islands now serve as breeding grounds for bald eagles and ospreys. We looked intently through our binoculars, thinking we might be able to report that we had seen one of these birds, but we were unrewarded. The fact that eagles did breed off City Point was a comforting thought, philosophically, since there was very little else to redeem it as a place for yachters to visit.

Leaving City Point, we quietly moved past tree-lined shores, making our way downriver with only a sand-moving barge for company. We identified Berkeley and Lower Brandon from the water, and did get excited at this first glimpse of the old mansions we were planning to visit. It was a full twelve hours from the time we had left that morning before we reached Kingsmill, where we had reserved a slip for the night. We had been particularly hoping for a good day of sailing, as we wanted to show the *Response* to her

Monitors at City Point

proper care and color. All of these monitors have seen service. They are part of the original fleet which settled in a practical way the value of armored ships. Weak as they are now from age and in comparison with the ironclads of other governments which have decent self-respect, they were once the very bulwarks of the nation.

Taking the James as a whole, the banks are still very much as nature and war left them. Considering that nearly three centuries have passed since the early colonists landed, it is remarkable how many of the beautiful building-sites along the banks remain timber-clad to this day. Here and there a stately mansion rises on the bluffs or towers up from behind the belt of woods.

The same old tale of timber destruction which is written on the bare hillsides of the North is being rewritten on the banks of the James. Timber exportation is one of the industries of the region,—

Mothball fleet in James River

best advantage to our friend, John Grosso. A pilot, sailor, photographer, and the closest of friends, John had driven in from Philadelphia to meet us at the First Colony dock. We had done a good bit of Caribbean sailing together in the past, and it felt good to have him "back on board" with us for a few days on the Chesapeake. When we stopped for the night, there still wasn't any air, and we were glad for the amenities of the marina. After longed-for showers, we had dinner overlooking the fairways of this resort and residential community. The next day, we "vacationed," spending a fun-filled day at Busch Gardens Amusement Park, irresistible because it was only a couple of miles away.

On arriving back at the marina, we discovered that Moses had made an abortive attempt to explore the dock. Curiosity is a characteristic trait of many other living creatures besides cats, but there is little doubt that felines display a consistent knack of getting in curiosity's way. Mose was found by the dockmaster, Jeff

National Cemetery at City Point

good enough for the present, but, in the interest of the future, not nearly so productive of benefit as a policy would be which made men save that timber where it is and gain the year's living from old acres better tilled. Three-fourths of all the vessels that went out of the James during our stay there were freighting away timber. Granting what must be granted,—the unhealthiness of the low grounds,—would it not be better to leave them for the present in standing timber, where it exists, or even to replant where it has been removed in anticipation of the time, which is surely coming, in which forest value will be as certain as the value of a silver-mine?

The difference between the season here and near Philadelphia is quite marked. As I looked from my cabin window on June 20th I could see much of the wheat crop already cut and "in shock." A day earlier I had found blackberies (*Rubus villosus*) fully ripened;

72

Hopewell off City Point

Eberhard, clinging tenaciously to a mooring line, meowing loudly
and a bit fearfully. He rescued her and took her into the office to
await our return; there she ungraciously stretched out in Jeff's
chair and went to sleep. It has been said that in the past certain
breeds of cats were regarded as sacred and that each cat had its
own servant, who was liable to severe punishment if anything
untoward happened to its master or mistress. Folklore or not, we
can only say that cats, especially kittens, enslave the attention of
those around them, and thus it was that Mose had spent the
evening monopolizing everyone's attentions. We became convinced that she was probably putting it on a bit about the rescue
mission and making the most of it. Another of Mose's adventures
coming to a happy conclusion!

Early the next morning John regretfully departed, and we
moved on with great-grandfather's itinerary—to Berkeley for a
visit to the old mansion house which, erected in 1726, has been

A stray shot in Norfolk Harbor

even the wild plums (*Prunus Americana*) were commencing to be edible.

With a fair wind, on June 20th we left City Point to descend the river. The first stopping-place was at Berkeley, a few miles below. I wanted a view of the old mansion-house, which, erected in 1723, has been the scene of many important historical events. Tradition tells us that on the lawn in front of this building Patrick Henry rehearsed his great speech to the Virginia representatives, before whom it was in form delivered at the Virginia Convention. In the same house President Harrison was born. It was used also by General McClellan during his Peninsular campaign; and then were removed the beautiful trees which once ornamented the

74

Machine in Norfolk Harbor

Berkeley

lawn, facing and gradually sloping to the river, three hundred yards away.

The steep banks of the bluff, where they face the river, show a mixture of sand and gravel which is very like that revealed by the cuts of the Chesapeake and Delaware Canal. The bald cypress (*Taxodium distichum*) was at its very best when I saw it in June. Its light-green feathery foliage contrasted richly with the dark-hued pines back of it. To those who have never seen these trees before, they always present a strange appearance, which is due, first, to the fact that they grow down to and in the water; and, second, to their large, conical, buttress-like hollow roots. They can hardly help enlarging one's view of the possibilities of plant-life and form for variation. Along-side of or but little higher than the cypress, the buttonwood (*Platanus occidentalis*), with its large leaves, was

the scene of many historical events. The land on which the mansion stands was part of a grant made in 1619 by King James I to the Berkeley Company, and it was the place where the first Thanksgiving Day was celebrated in Virginia. In the same house, two presidents, William Henry Harrison, "Old Tippecanoe," and Benjamin Harrison, were born. During the War between the States, as it is referred to in this part of the country, General Daniel Butterfield composed "Taps" at Berkeley. We learned all of this when, as guests of the plantation, we attended a slide presentation and took a subsequent tour of the house conducted by Mrs. Roberta Luce, a most entertaining hostess. After the guided portion of our visit was concluded, we were free to tour the grounds on our own. It was difficult to capture the placid and changeless charm of Berkeley in a set of photographs or in words. We did have the good fortune of spending some time with Mr. Malcolm Jamieson, the present owner of Berkeley Plantation. This hospitable gentleman spent an hour with us, sharing the excitement of our project, and answering our questions. He made us a gift of *The Great Plantation,* a recently published book on Berkeley, which provides delightful reading about the glorious episodes of American history that have been enacted on its premises.

From Berkeley, we journeyed to the doorstep of what today is known as Lower Brandon, arriving on June 22, exactly one hundred years to the day of great-grandfather's visit. Lower Brandon was like stepping into another world, a world of peace and permanence, where on the face of it everything moved slowly and deliberately, in time with the even-flowing river.

In the absence of Mr. and Mrs. Robert Daniel, present owners, we, like great-grandfather, were received by a lady of the house, Miss Cunningham. This gentlewoman was the social secretary to the senior Mrs. Daniel, and continued to reside with the household. Although born in 1899, she is as fit in body and mind as someone half her age, and she spent much time with us, showing us the home inside and out. We were delighted to learn new historical facts and stories not mentioned by great-grandfather.

thriving luxuriantly; and, still farther from the river, the leaves of the *Liquidambar*, or the sweetgum tree, stood out boldly with their five to seven projecting ray-like lobes.

Our short stay on the James would, of course, furnish very incomplete data on which to base an estimate as to the number of vessels of considerable size which pass up and down the river each day. While we were there, probably it would be safe to say, there were three or four daily each day that went or had been above City Point.

On the evening of June 20th we anchored near what was left of the old Fort Powhatan. A still strong river-wall is all that marks the site of this once-important post from the river side. A country store stands on the hill above, and a wharf furnishes a landing-place for good-sized vessels. Shipment of timber appears to be the chief industry. Earthworks, occupied for a time during the recent war, are on the hill back.

Continuing our voyage down the river, the next landing was made at Lower Brandon. During the war I had occasion to know the bravery and persistency of purpose with which the Virginians adhered to their doctrine of State Rights. Here, at Lower Brandon, for the first time in my life, I was made acquainted with the hospitality for which the old families of the State are so proverbial. I presented myself at the door of the noble old mansion, a sun-browned yachtsman, certainly with dust on my shoes, and I fear with the odor of tar on my raiment. The gentleman of the house being away, permission to photograph the house and its surroundings was very kindly given by the ladies. By them, also, I was taken to the parlor and shown the old family portraits, each of which had a history. Indeed, it is very doubtful if a single private room on the continent contains a larger number of portraits of distinguished persons, most of whom, too, were related to the occupants of the house. Some of these paintings were more than a century and a half old. Colonel Byrd, who figured so conspicuously in all of the early doings of the colony and in its relation to the mother-country, had, of course, a conspicuous place among the family portraits. Mrs. H. kindly allowed me to examine the origi-

For example, there was a wedding band that had been found in the ceiling, the mystery of it never resolved but evoking the memory of a tragic romance associated with a beautiful, former mistress, Miss Evelyn Byrd. In and out of the house we went, exploring the bullet marks on the eastern front of the mansion, the scars of two wars. During the Revolution, a British ship fired on Brandon; but the damage was minimal compared to what was done by Federal soldiers who occupied the building and used a good portion of the paneling from the living room for firewood. An ancient brick "Block House" that Miss Cunningham described as a place where the family hid from Indian raids still stands. The main house was designed by Thomas Jefferson, and has two ancient, gnarled wisteria that are purported to be a favorite haunting place for the mansion ghost. The gardens, too, testify to the passing of many generations, having among them very large dwarf boxwoods and giant hardwoods. The crepe myrtle has grown to extraordinary heights, and it is not surprising that Brandon is included on the tour for Prince George County's Garden Week. The river is some three hundred yards from the house, creating a vista which drew our attention. There at the river's edge was a majestic, one-hundred-year-old urn. Suddenly, standing there, we felt humble, diminished as individuals in the face of all that had taken place here.

At Lower Brandon, we received the same kind of graciousness we had come to associate with Virginia plantation owners. We were allowed to stroll through the grounds and gardens, delighted to behold and to trace the same paths great-grandfather had taken from the waterfront, and around the plantation. We were grateful too for the traditions that have been kept and cherished in these great homes along the James River.

On the next day, we photographed the mouth of the Chickahominy River. It was an idyllic morning, the sun shining and wind in the sail. The camera revealed nothing of the turbulence that had taken place on this river during the Revolutionary War, when the British ran along the timbered shores intent on destroying the Chickahominy shipyard. We were tempted to go on up the Chick-

Brandon—Old dwelling house

nal manuscript account by Colonel Byrd of running the line between Virginia and North Carolina. He was himself one of the leading characters in the work. Colonel Byrd's writings furnish a mine of wealth which no history student of the times and the colony can afford to be without. They have been published under the title of "The Westover Papers," and throughout are characterized by elegance, force, and reliability.

Colonel William Byrd was a rich planter, whose multifold activities and varied accomplishments recall that generation of Englishmen to which Virginia owed her origin. Educated in England, then called to the bar and elected a fellow of the Royal Society, afterward for thirty-seven years a councillor in Virginia, three times agent at the English court, and the leading spirit in

ahominy, on a reach with a good stiff breeze, but resisted this
temptation to vary from our schedule.

Jamestown Island below the Chickahominy was the next point
on our itinerary. Unlike great-grandfather, we had no access to
the island from the water; we found a marina and rented a car to
take us on this leg of the trip. Dr. Ransom True, Research Histori-
an of the Association for the Preservation of Virginia Antiquities
(known as APVA), received us with the utmost interest, and
allowed us to take up a goodly portion of his day with our inquiries
and taking photographs. His patience, kindness, and enthusiasm
continued after we reached home, as we corresponded with him
over some points that had interested us both.

We especially wanted to secure good photographs of the restored
Jamestown Island, because in 1883 even the ruins had almost
disappeared. During the course of this cruise we developed a
sincere admiration for great-grandfather's prophetic visions and
his zeal for the preservation of trees and woodlands. During his
lifetime he was considered the father of Pennsylvania forestry and
founded the Pennsylvania State Forest Academy in Mont Alto.
His concerns about the future were congruent with the objectives
of APVA, which has been the owner, preserver, and administrator
of the Jamestown Island National Historic Site since 1892.

The photographs we took in 1983 show the remarkable results
achieved by APVA. The partially ruined brick church tower,
erected after 1647, stands eighteen feet square, with walls three
feet thick at its base. Standing beside it is a brick memorial
church, inside of which are the remains of the brick and cobblestone frame from the 1617 church. It is believed that in this
primitive church John Rolfe and Pocahontas were married. It is a
romantic tradition, but when inside the church, one is moved
with a hushed respect to think of the ideals that pertain to the
founding of our nation.

Portraits of Colonel and Miss Eveline Byrd

every industrial enterprise, Byrd shows us how active and brilliant a career lay open to a great Virginia landholder.

It is, then, to Byrd's industry in recording the events of his daily life that his own well-established claim to historical remembrance is due. Besides this, however, these same labors made him the first American historical authority of his times, and also the preserver of a knowledge of social life which but for him must have been in great part lost. Along with his high sense of humor and a most keen penetration, he appears to have been, withal, somewhat caustic in his writings.

The portrait of Colonel Byrd, and also that of Miss Eveline Byrd, hang on the parlor wall at Lower Brandon. The latter must have been strikingly beautiful. The impression she produced has almost become historical.

Ordinarily, we associate a walk through a cemetery with ghost stories and Halloween. However, a walk through the cemetery at Jamestown Island is a walk through history. The grave markers, carefully protected from curiosity seekers, not only give information about individuals, but reveal much about a society's view of death at that particular time. We spent a few moments in the daylight, surrounded by the green of summer, reading and interpreting the grave markers, a decidedly unscary experience.

The lone cypress, as it is referred to today, stood like a silent sentinel as we wandered through the site; the magnolia was in full bloom, and its fragrance seemed to temper the afternoon air. We sat awhile at the riverside, sharing our lunch with the squirrels and birds. These creatures were nothing like those in downtown Philadelphia who command you to feed them or chatter in annoyance at you if you don't. The Virginia squirrels, a cardinal, and gulls that sat in attendance on our luncheon did so quietly and unobtrusively, waiting for whatever might come their way by an accidental or deliberate hand.

The seawall where the birds perched dates from 1901; the pilings extending out from the seawall date from 1895. The old magazine is now under water, but the spot is redolent of patriotic and sacred memories. The entire site is well maintained. Park rangers serve as guides, or the visitor can take a newly developed walking tour whose points of interest are marked by anodized aluminum plaques that provide information in an attractive way, appropriate to the setting.

When we awoke the next morning, the cabin was filled with sunlight; it was a warm and friendly sanctum from which we could venture happily to whatever the day held. We got ready, rather languorously, then headed downriver, passing Hog Island, gazing intently at the Point of Shoals Lighthouse. We did not anchor there, finding nothing inviting about attempting a geological collection since we did not even know vaguely what "pectin and its usual associates" might be.

Brandon—Parlor

Nothing struck me so forcibly as the dignified and frank manner in which the war and its immediate issues have been accepted by the property holders along the James. There is a nobility which is above even the reverses of war, and if ever in my life I felt that I was in the presence of such it was at Lower Brandon. I would like to say more, but deprive myself of the pleasure, lest the sincerity of what I have written should be doubted.

I was particularly anxious to secure a good photograph of the Lower Brandon mansion-house. But here, as on Jamestown Island, the two places where, of all others, I most desired success, I absolutely failed to obtain the views. The mansion is composed of two wings and a main central building. The wings were erected first, and of bricks brought over from England. One finds there the same alternating order of red and black bricks that can still be

Later, when we had completed the cruise, we pursued our investigation of the nature and location of great-grandfather's specimens from that part of the James. This took place in Philadelphia at the Academy of Natural Sciences. We learned that the specimens were, indeed, catalogued and housed there, in the department of malacology. Pleasantly surprised, we arranged with Dr. Carol Jones, the curator, to visit the museum and view the collection. She was happy to take us into the archives where, carefully and gently, she delivered pieces of the collection from a drawer, amongst rows and rows of similar drawers. We gazed with an extraordinary intensity at one of the shells, expecting to be moved or inspired, perhaps, by its age or familial associations. We did not, I am sorry to admit, feel moved by what we saw; it was rather a large and unappealing specimen, which we duly photographed. That great-grandfather's collection was saved for these hundred years was not unusual; Dr. Jones explained it was a matter of historical interest since such a collection enabled the scientist to study patterns of evolution, examine changes over time, and record natural extinction. We were impressed by this enthusiastic interest in fossils from the Chesapeake Bay, significantly enhancing our final views of the shells themselves.

Our run to Newport News was not a tedious one. Under the Hampton Roads Bridge we had a current that was giving us a two-knot "kick in the rear" to help us on our way. The coal loaders we photographed were in stark contrast to the pictures of the Old Dominion we had so recently been viewing. Gone were the stillness, the gentle melancholy charm of an ageless past. Instead, there were, lining the shore, large conveyances for unloading freight cars onto ships. Everything seemed vital, alive as if ready almost to spring into action.

We stopped for the night in Hampton Creek at the Hampton Yacht Club. Here we made the unfortunate discovery that we had lost our two-horsepower outboard; it had been taken, safety line and all, off the back of the dinghy in all of the yawling about we had

seen in so many of the older parts of Philadelphia. Subsequently the main central building, as it stands to-day, joined the wings. In spite of the injury wrought by war, it is a most imposing building. Inside all was once in keeping with the exterior; that it is not so now is largely due to some unjustifiable acts of vandalism, I am ashamed to say, on the part of our own Northern troops.

I had the pleasure of accompanying the ladies to the harvest-field, where Major Page was superintending the cutting of the wheat crop. I found him a courteous gentleman, who shook hands very cordially with me knowing that we were on different sides of the recent conflict.

There were on the estate about two hundred and fifty acres in wheat, and some eighty laborers engaged in harvesting it. The major suggested about eighteen bushels per acre as the probable yield of the one-hundred-acre field he was then engaged upon. In the thriving crop of clover I could see the sign of a restored fertility. The absence of this on much of the land that I visited along the James was leading me to underestimate the recuperative process which is taking place.

Lower Brandon mansion, along with its large-hearted hospitality, is a house of "many industries," as one of the ladies remarked. It is the post-office for the region, and the money received for their service to their country is set apart for the church there, which, like many others, needs all it can obtain to enable it vigorously to prosecute its Christian work.

If to the occupants Lower Brandon appears like a "Paradise Lost" since the war, there are many who hope that ere long it may be a "Paradise Regained." I visited the grounds early in the morning of June 22nd. The cooing of the pigeons and the whistle of the partridges were everywhere heard. Squirrels played among the branches, or deliberately sat and chattered at me as I passed. Their only fear seemed to be when on the ground; but, once on the tree, they immediately stopped to inspect the intruder. The *Magnolia grandiflora* was in full bloom, and its fragrance appeared to temper the morning air. Mimosas, with their delicate foliage and still more delicate flowers, peeped out from under the

Dr. Rothrock's fossils

done rounding Newport News. After exclamations of concern, punctuated with the appropriate nautical oaths, we set out to replace it. It was a short walk to the Hampton Yacht Yard, where we purchased a new outboard. We filled up, tested it, and made sure it was affixed to the stern with a new safety line. We were, perhaps, a little compulsive about having things on board in their place and readied for immediate use. Although we sometimes reminded ourselves of refugees perpetually on the move, it was more a matter of safety afloat and vigilance than a personality disorder.

One thing that we noticed about having a tabby as a crew member was that everyone who saw Mose, a domestic American short haired breed, was reminded of a cat they once knew, had, or had left at home. She made quick friends among fellow yachters,

87

Brandon—Front lawn

taller trees. Honeysuckles twined everywhere about the mansion, taking possession of whatever they could embrace.

Before leaving Lower Brandon and its associations, I must call attention to the bullet-marks on the eastern front of the mansion. These are but a partial expression of the lawlessness of our own troops. The shots were fired not in battle, but represent the ungoverned lawlessness of warfare. I do not mean to assert that our own soldiers were worse than others, but simply to say that all such acts as mutilate property, destroy life, or in any way injure an individual, unless done (as these were not) in execution of military duty, are wholly inexcusable and unjustifiable under any pretext whatever. There is a still worse tale of vandalism to be told in

88

Urn at Brandon

and we were becoming quite used to being asked her name, age, and gender, explaining why a "she" cat had a "he" name, and finally, introducing ourselves in the aftermath of introducing her. Not one passerby who noticed Mose on deck failed to follow up with a friendly greeting or comment. That friendliness is inherent in the nature of yachtsmen there is no doubt; the process just became easier with our little tabby initiating, in her way, the conversation.

After dinner at the yacht club, we walked to the store for a Sunday paper and a favorite treat—an ice-cream cone. Back on board, we enjoyed the prelude to nightfall, sitting on deck. Cool and quiet, the early evening is a favorite time of day for us when

89

connection with the same building. On one of the windows there was, written by himself, the name of each President, down to that of our martyred Lincoln. Associated with these were the autographs of many statesmen and scholars. One might suppose that such honored autographs would be secure, engraved with the diamond on the glass, against even the great destroyer Time, and that they would be both sacred and safe among the soldiers of Freedom. But they were neither, for an unpalsied Northern arm shattered the pane and destroyed the roll.

River navigation is always most uncertain. How often we were "headed off" by the wind in some days of sailing on the James is hardly possible to say. We started to Brandon in a calm, but reached our anchorage in a furious little gale, which covered the river with white-caps in a few minutes. However, the tide was going out, and we soon found the yacht had nestled down in a soft bed of mud, where she quietly lay. That was not a hundred yards distant from where an ocean-steamer had passed an hour before.

On the evening of June 22nd we anchored south of the Chickahominy, and next morning ran over to photograph the mouth of this historic river. In itself it is nothing but a good-sized stream, opening through swamps and low, pine-covered bluffs into the James. For all this, however, it has been the scene of some of the most important events witnessed in our short colonial and federal life. Captain John Smith, very soon after the location of the settlers upon Jamestown Island, set out to explore the Chickahominy region, which, though nominally under the control of Powhatan, was directly governed by his brother Opechancanough, who from the first to last was hostile to the whites. It was on this trip that Smith was captured, and marched from village to village by his captors, then doomed to execution, and rescued from the jaws of death by Pocahantas. This, at least, is the legend.

The bluffs, along the southern shore especially, furnished a most instructive lesson in world-making, stratum after stratum being piled each above the other in a very striking way, their horizontal position suggesting naturally enough their deposition

cruising. We sat, contented and relaxed, eyes half-closed, impressed with the visage of the setting sun. We felt like two of the richest people in the world. It was our time for not thinking about anything at all; just being there defined our existence—our minds and bodies loitering on a holiday, to emerge renewed and serene. If everyone could have moments of this pervading kind of peace, there would be no threat of nuclear annihilation; who would dare risk not ever having such an hour of earth, sky, and water, with its healing tranquillity?

The next morning our friends, Sally and Clyde Harbison, with their son Greg, joined us to go up the York River. We made a late start, and at two-thirty rounded Tue Marshes Tower, which is visible for eight miles to the approaching yachter. The day was hazy and hot; with a wind that could hardly be called favorable, we motor-sailed, averaging four and a half to five knots. We were fascinated by the numerous fishing nets clustered together, with an assortment of bay birds sharing perches on the poles—herons, osprey, and gulls—all eyeing the nets in anticipation of lunch. We had never fished from our boat, although we had heard friends talk enthusiastically about the easily available, fine fishing in the southern bay. It sounded quite simple when they talked about trailing a line through a school of blues, but the notion of carrying bait, reels, poles, and lures made it seem simpler to buy a fish than to catch one. Nonetheless, the York River was a tempting place to fish, and if we had had any of the requisite apparatus, we would have been sorely tempted to give it a try.

When we arrived at the York River Yacht Haven, we must have looked like a boat with a limp, dejected sail. It had been, unfortunately, an uninspiring trip in terms of being able to share good sailing with our friends. In spite of this, we had enjoyed ourselves. There is something special about being on a boat deck; it is an open, airy place, with no walls to keep life out. When you sit there, the sun, even on a cloudy day, seems to be in your soul.

Brandon—Bullet holes

from the water, and then, being undisturbed ever since. On the other hand, the water, I might say, gives an equally interesting lesson, but one which is not so far advanced. Approaching the southern shore, just below Hog Island, as we were hunting a channel into a little creek, we found by the lead-line that for a long distance the bottom was almost absolutely flat. "One fathom" was the report, repeated until it became painfully monotonous. The lead indicated everywhere that soft mud was being evenly deposited. In many places an oar could be run down into it several feet with the utmost ease. The bluffs were once just as the river-bed now is, and allowing sufficient time, the future student of geology may find the now-forming mud flats above the surface of the water, and point to them as being simply another page in the same natural history.

Bullet holes at Brandon

After a quick dinner, we explored our surroundings, finding the York River Yacht Haven a very complete facility for the visiting boater. Slips with electricity, a laundromat, a ship's store with a trading library, a pool, showers, and car rental—all on site—are a bit rare. We were pleased that we had come to the place. We also discovered that friends from home, Brent and Anne Follweiler, whom we were to meet later up the Bay, bought their first boat here. We parted with the Harbisons, delighted at the quick and easy friendship that had sprung up between us. It was clear that we would make a point of rendezvousing with them in the years to come.

We woke early the next morning to a beautiful day. But as we got ready for our departure, we discovered that Mose was not on board. A quick search of the dock area did not turn up our cat, and

93

Jamestown Island was the next point of interest below the Chickahominy. Mr. Brown, the present proprietor of Old Jamestown, received me with the utmost kindness, and allowed me to photograph whatever I desired to. The patience of gentlemen who own such interesting spots as this passes my comprehension. I had no letters of introduction anywhere; and I take this opportunity of saying, once and for all, that the pleasantest memories of my trip on the James are associated with the uniform kindness I received from those upon whom I called for information, or for permission to photograph points of interest. I especially desired to secure good photographs of the ruins on Jamestown Island. My want of success has been explained in connection with a similar failure at Lower Brandon.

Even the ruins of Jamestown have almost disappeared. Fragments of the old magazine remain, and also a portion of the church tower; but these, with the cemetery back of the church, are the only visible memories of a time and a settlement which we regret left so few monuments. It is evident, however, from the scattered bricks and the faint indications of old cellars and the like, that the settlement covered a considerable area.

The most interesting ruin of Old Jamestown is, of course, its church tower. One marvels that a church so large as this was (judging from the ruined tower) could have been erected at so early a period in colonial history. It is to be remembered that to the men of those times (at least, to the better part of them) worship was something more than a luxury. I did not measure the tower (as I should have done), but should say it had a square base of about twenty feet. The remains still rise twenty-five feet, and are entered by a fine large doorway. The bricks, of course, were brought over from England. The first question which naturally suggests itself is: Why should a spot so full of sacred and patriotic memories as this is be allowed to fall into ruin, and to be overgrown with weeds? Or, worse, why should it be allowed to remain so? Alas for mankind! The proprietor apologized for the appearance of the ground and said, "I would gladly open it up and uncover the graves, were it not for the fact that to do so would simply be to

York River scene

what had started out as casual concern became real anxiety. At that moment a gentleman from the boat next to ours approached saying, "I think we've got your cat on board. She's asleep on the shoulder of my boy." He told us that they had returned late to their boat the evening before, that his son noticed our captivating cat washing herself on our cabin, and began playing with her. Mose, finding this young man a better companion than her sleeping owners, abandoned ship. Relieved, we returned to the *Response* to finish getting ready, laughing at her impertinence and at our initial dismay. She must have heard our voices, for we could hear plaintive meowing. Coming out on deck, we found Mose searching for a place to board. We pulled the boat in close to the dock, offering her encouragement and confidently, with rather more grace than we expected, she leaped on board. Presumably, she found it more pleasing to breakfast with us than to sleep with

95

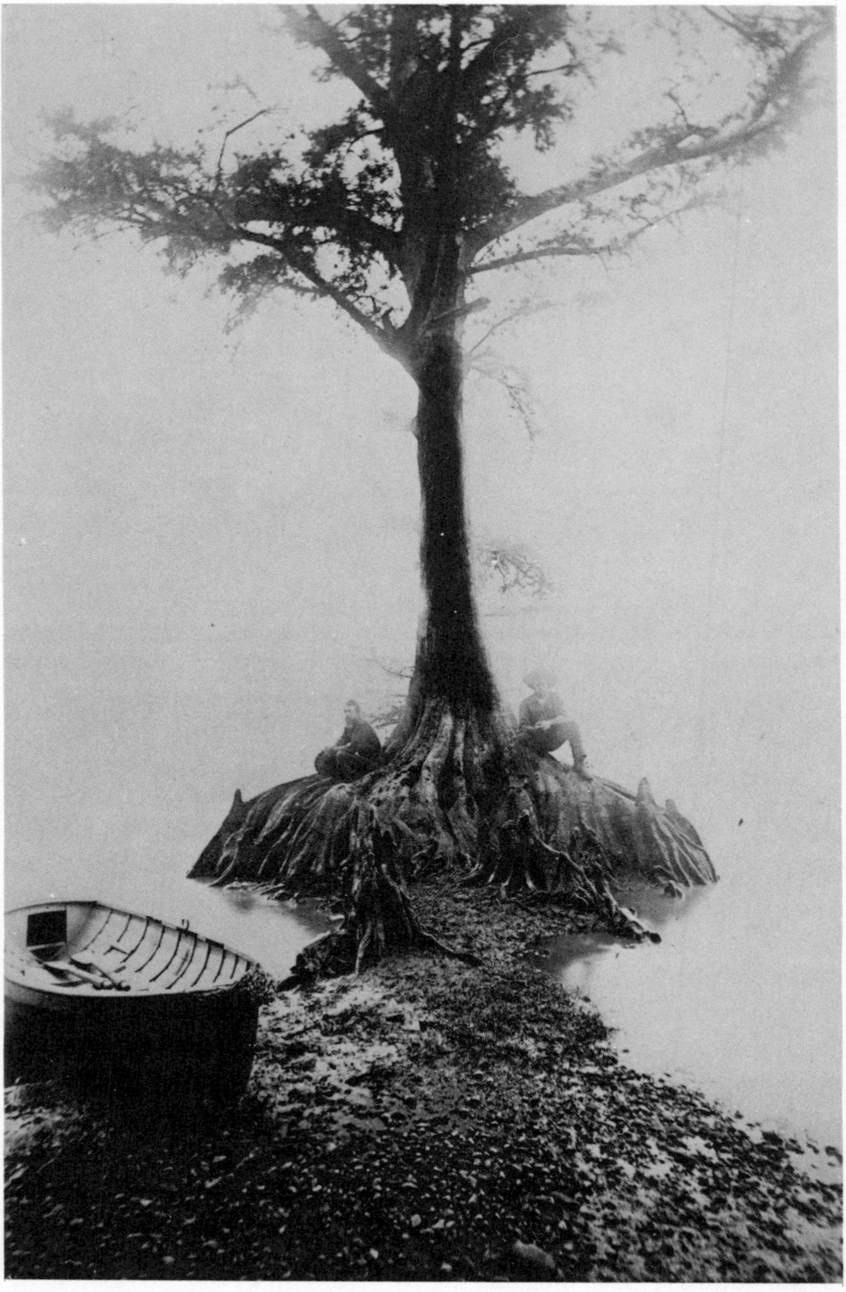

A cypress tree

Cypress trees in James River

make them more accessible to curiosity-seekers. Men come to the old tower and carry off the young ivy shoots; they break the tombstones, and nothing is so sacred as to prevent its destruction." From what I saw, there could be no doubt about the truth of this statement.

Through the gateway of the tower we passed into the old graveyard, over what was probably the site of the body of the church. Here and there an opening in the rank underbrush and weeds revealed a tombstone or sepulchral slab, and on some of these an inscription may be made out. Time has dealt harshly with the lettering, and in some cases almost destroyed the characters. I copied the following inscription:

Under this Stone lies interred
The Body of
Mrs. Hannah Ludwell
Relict of
The Hon. Phillip Ludwell, Esq.
By whom She has left
One Son and Two Daughters
After a most exemplary Life
Spent in cheerful Innocence
And exercise of
Piety, Charity, and Hospitality
She Patiently submitted to
Death on the 4th Day of April, 1731, in the 52
Year of Her Age.

Another reads:

Here Lyeth William Sherwoo--d, [?]
That Was Born in the Parish
of White Chapel Near
London. A Great Sinner
Waiting for a Joyfull
Resurrection.

her new companion. So, the transfer of loyalty was made, and she rejoined us to continue traveling the Bay.

Leaving York River Yacht Haven, we again noticed the nets, now being tended by industrious fishermen. There too were the not-so-industrious blue heron, who perched with watchful stillness, waiting for a morning catch to come their way. We would have liked to see an osprey or another bay bird come upon a school of fish upon which to feed. We have seen these birds cruise overhead or work a bank in search of their prey. In spite of the fact that our knowledge of ornithology was limited, we enjoyed speculating about the ways of these creatures, and were never bored.

Our chart indicated a swash channel which would enable us to head up toward New Point Comfort. With clear skies and excellent visibility, we passed the abandoned New Point Comfort lighthouse. In the calm peace of a summer morning, the lighthouse, a white alabaster tower set down in the middle of a concrete island, appeared like a bride of the land. There is a kind of outraged purity about these abandoned lighthouses. We have heard rumors that some of the lighthouses will be sold, either to museums or private owners. In any event we hope that they will be preserved and not left indecently to crumble and disintegrate.

There is a beach around behind New Point Comfort which one can take a dinghy to, being careful of the current. Because we would soon have both current and wind against us as we headed up the Bay, we relinquished the idea of a picnic luncheon there in favor of an early arrival in Antipoison Creek. This part of our journey emphasized the need for a sharp lookout as well as up-to-date charts and a fathometer. Crab pots and fish nets covered the water like the leaves of fall; they were everywhere, and we could not leave the tiller to an autohelm in such waters. The binoculars became a fixed item on deck when we were underway in the western part of the Chesapeake.

Rounding Wolfe Trap, our compass read 005, a clear indication of our northward heading. A couple of hours later, by Windmill Point, we photographed a workboat with its full load of oysters. The day's bounty covered even the cabin front, and how

Jamestown Island—Old church tower

Church tower at Jamestown

A few hundred yards above the church tower, along the bank of the river, we came upon what tradition calls the "old magazine." I at first thought I had reason for doubting that this had been its purpose. However, a closer examination showed me that the tradition was probably correct. The vault and the thickness of the walls make this the most plausible theory. The photograph shows that the building is now almost wholly undermined by the water. A cypress-tree, still farther up, stands now well out in the water. This, too, the photograph shows. Yet, some thirty years ago, the road, I was told, ran by that tree; hence so recently as this the magazine must have been well inland. These data serve to show with what rapidity the river is encroaching upon the land.

Passing Hog Island on our way down, we ran in along-shore, and spent Sunday at anchor near Ferguson's wharf, which is nearly abreast of the Point of Shoals light-house.

The bluffs looked very inviting, and I expected to find something of interest there. We had seen a blue stratum exposed at several points along the river. Here it formed the base of the bluffs, and was very suggestive of tertiary deposits, which I had seen elsewhere. However, Lew anticipated me in the discovery. He soon returned to the yacht with the news that there was no end of such things (coral and fossil shells) on shore. I suggested that the coral might have come there as ballast from the West Indies; but Lew scouted the idea: "There is too much of it for that." So we went ashore together. The blue stratum was full of shells (pectin and its usual associates). Here and there the tide had undermined it, and masses fell to the tide-level, where the shells lay in profusion. The coral revealed itself just at the tide-line, and not in the bluff, but out in the water. So far as we could see, it was there as an immense mass, from which we broke off a fragment weighing about two hundred pounds. It never came there as ballast. As to its origin and its extent geologists may decide, if, indeed, they have not already done so long since. We—that is, Lew and I—made considerable collections of these interesting things for the Philadelphia Academy of Natural Sciences.

Oyster boat

the captain could see to navigate was a mystery. For the past few hours, we had been free of any course obstacles but as we tried to find our way into Fleets Bay, which required a good search, the inevitable crab pots began to reappear. Never having been known to grumble when presented with a bowl of fresh crab meat, we attempted to keep our perspective about the nuisance of the *pots*, which appeared to port and starboard with annoying persistence.

After an hour exploring Antipoison Creek, we decided to pit great-grandfather's judgment about its desirability as an anchorage against the *Mid-Atlantic Waterway Guide*, which suggested that Indian Creek might be prettier. We had, actually, a number

Jamestown—Old magazine

June 25th gave us a strong head-wind, which, with the tide against us, made the run to Newport News a tedious one. No stop was made there as we had "done the place" on our way up the river.

Newport News appears to be one of the spots created for some great ends. The great depth of water along-shore, its accessibility (being free from ice the year through), and, above all, its being midway between the lands of wheat and cotton, are factors in its destiny which indicate a great future for the place. Add to these the fact that a strong railroad company is erecting buildings so large, so costly, and permanent that it cannot afford any failure on the part of the place.

The name Newport News is still full of stirring memories. For one short day the victory gained by the "Merrimac" ("Virginia")

104

Site of magazine, Jamestown

of anchorage choices. Dymer Creek, with a sandy beach, for example, had on one side of its entrance the ruins of an old fish factory. Although we were interested in photographing the crumbling remains of an old processing plant near a fishmill or its facsimile, what we really needed was ice and fuel, and so we headed for Indian Creek. At the Chesapeake Boat Basin we got the necessary items, as well as a new crab net used by us to retrieve the various items that occasionally go adrift on a boat. Our old one was in such disreputable condition, it might hold a cushion that went overboard, but nothing smaller; this purchase was to be a stroke of luck as later events proved.

Our next stop was the Rappahannock Oyster Company. Here we purchased some crab meat, wonderful large chunks of it,

awakened hopes among the Confederates which must have been bright,—the more so as all that had been expected of the new ironclad was far more than realized in her combat with our wooden vessels. These hopes were but bright illusions, for the next day the "Monitor" turned the tide of victory against the soldiers and the sailors of the South.

We anchored on the evening of the 25th of June in Hampton Creek, among "oyster-pungies" and fishing-canoes. As I watched the water in the night from the deck, one of the "nettle-fish" (jelly-fish) passed by, slowly drifting out with the tide. It was brilliant enough to be seen as a ball of phosphorescent light. We found them so abundant as to be nuisances. In Mob-jack Bay, north of York River, bathing-houses are built for the express purpose of protecting the bathers against them.

On the night of the 26th of June we had a settled rain. Even if there is no inspiration to me in the patter on the deck, it is always pleasant. In the "Marble Faun, " Hawthorne makes his count say, "The sky is an old roof, and no doubt the sins of mankind have made it gloomier than it used to be." It was a leaky roof that night, in all truth, but our deck was better than the roof; so that we had none of the count's gloomy philosophy in the little cabin. The next morning it was still raining.

But, take it "all in all," the life on the water is a healthy one. In spite of rain and wind and soul-tormenting calm, hardened hands and sunbrowned face, I have enjoyed it all. It is simply a return to first principles,—a vagabond life, if you insist upon so considering it, but still one which most men some time long for. June 1st I came on board painfully conscious of having nerves and aching points all over my body. But after a month of aquatic life I found muscle had the nerves in subjection, and not a single pain interfered with perfect peace of mind or of body.

How much these summer-loitering hours with earth and sky and water would renew our youth if we would allow our minds and bodies a holiday ungrudged! When a man, already rich, comes to endure labor, through the heat of summer and through the cold of

quickly forgetting how ungrateful we had been earlier about the crab pots that had supplied our meal. Crabs and oysters were everywhere. In the store, iced oysters, fresh crab, and crabcakes were available; outside, steamers, with stray crabs scuttling around in an attempt to escape their fate. Mose, perched on the anchor, stared with fascination at one escapee that was inching its way across oyster shells in her direction as it sought to find a hiding place. Mose looked ready to leap ashore to make the final determination as to whether or not this was friend or foe. At the crucial moment, an oysterman approached, commenting, "Naw, kitty, it'd be darn mean if we let that crab get ahold of you." He reached with a gloved hand and grabbed the fierce looking crab, claws splayed for attack, and flung it back in the water. Little did Mose know what woe would have resulted from an engagement with a Chesapeake Bay blue crab.

At last, with forty miles between us and our morning starting place, we dropped anchor in Pitmans Cove. It was early evening and there were two other boats sharing the tree-lined, dappled shoreline that was reflected in the quiet water of our resting place. In this idyllic surrounding, we took our showers, especially enjoying the warm water and smell of soap after a day's cruising. We had just completed this activity, luxuriously clean and unclothed, when Joe exclaimed, "The cat just fell overboard!" Astonished, I began to ask how he could know and then stopped, deciding that it was a silly question. With a towel clutched around me, I shot out of the cabin, shouting at Joe to forget his bathing trunks, which he was trying to struggle into. I furiously tried to unsnap the crab net with my left hand, and I'm not ambidextrous in the calmest of situations. Abandoning all modesty, I let the towel go and unloosened the net, crying, "Where is she? I can't see her." Unceremoniously, Joe took the net from my trembling hand, and said calmly, "I'll get her." With that, a pathetic looking, meowing, drenched animal soon was placed in my discarded towel and promptly photographed. Later, after a strong cup of tea, we laughed at this most recent of Mose's adventures, and acknowl-

winter, simply for the gain it brings, then he needs a force to drag him off for a season, to isolate him from the world, while he can contemplate some high ideal in art or in science, in philanthropy or in religion.

Hampton Roads and the region around is the veritable historic centre of the country. An accident gave the name, Point Comfort, to the sandy point where Fortress Monroe now stands. Driven by a heavy storm in July from the Piankatank, Captain John Smith found his first secure shelter under its protection. Hence the name, inspired by gratitude. But how often since has the same safe anchorage awakened similar conditions!

A delightful, easy southerly wind carried us up the shore, past Back River, which was once the scene of General Magruder's military operations. The ground is now devoted to labors more peaceful, more odorous, and more useful. An establishment for the extraction of oil from the small fish known as "moss-bunker" stands in sight from the bay. These fish swim in schools, and may be recognized by the dark color they give the surface water. The refuse remainder, left after extracting the oil, is ground up and forms the basis of a fertilizer which is in considerable demand by agriculturists. That the business is lucrative may be supposed from the vast number of vessels engaged in the capture of these fish. Almost every inlet of considerable size along-shore has one or more "fish-mills," where "the catch" is "worked up." How long the industry will last at the present rate of destruction of the fish is a problem which we cannot yet solve. Those engaged in the business did not mention to me any scarcity of fish. Indeed, at Newport News the James River appeared to be dotted over with the dark schools.

As noon of the 28th of June approached, we rounded Too's Point light-house, on the York River, and looked long and eagerly before we saw Yorktown. A mere glance at the bluffs, which front the river, would leave on the mind of an observer the impression that these and the ground back of them were an ideal battle-field.

Our Mose

edged that my father had not nicknamed me "Calamity Jane" for nothing.

We were awakened early the next morning by the discordant sound of a tugboat horn. One of the boats in the cove had swung around and blocked the tug from reaching a barge parked in a back recess. As the obstructors pulled anchor, we sleepily viewed the activity and exchanged opinions about the merits of early rising,

The evening of June 29th found us anchored in Antepoisen Creek,—that is, in the hook made by the northern shore, which is guarded by Rappahannock Spit light-house. What evil genius inspired those who named Mob-jack Bay, Sting-Ray Point, Antepoisen Creek? Our run had been only about thirty-five miles. The wind was fair, though most of the way very light. So far as I am able to say, I think that, during the month of June, morning and evening can generally be depended upon for a breeze from some quarter in the Chesapeake Bay. There is almost certainly a trying noon calm, during which the sun beats down with a most intense fervor. Squalls, to be dreaded, often come during June and July, and their usual time of appearance is towards evening. Our harbor in Antepoisen Creek was another of the many beautiful ones, such as we had hitherto found. Near its head we were completely landlocked and had about two fathoms of water under the bow,— just such a place as one can sleep most soundly in. There was no fear of anything.

A brilliant shooting-star darted across the sky in the early evening, and after it there were several others, but none so bright as was the first.

Lying on the ground, or on the deck of a vessel, one becomes acquainted with the sky. The longer he looks, the more unfathomable do its depths appear. The most distant stars seem on the hither side of space, shining out clear of their background, and leave on the mind the sense of a great void behind them, dark or blue from its vastness. A night without such meteors is rather rare, but we are so taken away from them by fatigue, or so shut out from heaven by slate and shingles, that we miss seeing their fiery trails when they journey inside the limits of our vision, and thus we think them something unusual. I have companions who have sought wisdom in the books until they are pale, and who have lost the elastic step one should have until his head silvered. They can name each star and tell its distance from the earth in miles, but they have never laid down and gone to sleep while looking up at them, and wondering, not studying, how big those stars were. I think these persons have missed an element of education which

none of which were positive at this moment. Nonetheless, we roused ourselves, brewed a pot of coffee, and felt infinitely better as its tantalizing aroma brought to mind more pleasant associations of morning. We were soon on our way, sailing off our anchor under jib, averaging five knots out in the open. Mose, unsurprisingly, was quite skittish about joining us on deck, and we left her to resolve her problem in her own time.

Two hours later we entered the Great Wicomico. Rounding Fleet Point, we headed up Cockrell Creek to Reedville. It was our intent to make a short exploratory trip, then continue on our homeward leg. We took the sails down, and under motor skirted the fish factories spewing smoke in great streams of grey that appeared to attack the blue horizon with ferocity. We motored on, beyond the tall smokestack, finding some tranquil creeks and coves where one could enjoy a quiet anchorage. Turning around, we came out and made a little way upriver, past Sandy Point. The boat traffic had been minimal all week; it was only today, as the weekend approached, that other sailboats joined us here in Northern Virginia. At Horn Harbor, we headed back out, past Mill Creek, and ate lunch, musing about coming back sometime to the Great Wicomico to explore in leisure what for us had been an untraveled area of the Chesapeake Bay. Because we had stopped at Solomons on the way down, we opted to depart from great-grandfather's itinerary a bit, and make a stop in Crisfield on Tangier Sound.

In Tangier Sound, we followed the channel markers carefully, keeping an easy eleven feet of water underneath us. Although accustomed as we had become to the fascinations of the Bay, we could not resist observing and photographing the portside spectacle of watermen—and some waterwomen—busily tending their floats; the peelers within would soon become the much enjoyed softshell crabs. I could remember very well the first time I was served a softshell crab, being, then, a young Pennsylvanian uninitiated to such delicacies. I eyed it askance, wondering how on earth I would be able to eat it, but dutiful daughter that I was, I would try because I had been taught it was not polite to refuse to

would send them back to work wiser and better and healthier for their gazing.

"Crabbed" is a word the meaning of which I should enlarge, and say it is a senseless pugnacity and a disposition to attack anything with or without hope of success. This I would deduce from observations at headquarters. Lew brought a crab to the surface, which, though the well-baited hook was less than a foot away, was, nevertheless, attacking the lead sinker with all his might. Probably on reaching the bottom the sinker had fallen on his back or touched one of his numerous appendages, and thus excited his wrath, or he may have attacked it on the general principle that it was an intruder. When the water was clear and quiet, looking over the side of the boat, we saw another wrestling with a fish larger than itself. Their odd projecting eyes are sharp enough, and ever on the watch for something to attack. The first approach of an enemy causes the claws to rise in aggressive as well as defensive warfare. The crab is a mail-clad bully. Probably the fact that he is mail-clad, and hence more than a match for all his familiar associates, makes him reckless in attacking even those with whom he is not so well acquainted. He does not know that a falling brick would crush him, armor and all.

Crabs serve to reinforce some ideas one occasionally gets of men,—the less brains, as a rule, the more pugnacious,—that is, granting that all stomachs are equally good. I am persuaded that an angel would quarrel when suffering from dyspepsia.

Though we had a gun on board, no song-bird was shot, or even fired at, from my boat. We had every morning what was to me a sacred concert. Blackbirds, robins, sparrows, even crows and fish-hawks, joined as best they could in the chorus which was sure to bring the sleepers on deck. Is a man the worse for having emotions? Since then their notes sound to me so much like music intended for the best part of men that I always stop to listen. At all events, the soul capable of such enjoyment is somewhat the purer for being gratified.

On June the 30th we started early, hoping to make the harbor in the mouth of the Patuxent. This was only about forty-five miles

Crab pots

eat what you were served as a dinner guest. My plan of action was to take a small piece and then swallow it down with a mouthful of water. Tentatively I put the piece in my mouth, began to perfunctorily chew it, and discoverd a plump, moist piece of delicious meat. Since then, I have been a devotee of the sautéed softshell, often quietly amused at my mother's wisdom and prosaic advice, "You'll never know if you like something unless you try it."

We headed into Somers Cove, finding fuel and a slip at the Somers Cove Marina. Across the cove, a solitary catamaran had dropped anchor in the lee of the Coast Guard station, obviously disdaining spending a night at the dock. On the other hand, we were enticed by the idea of dinner at the Captain's Galley, one of our favorite restaurants on the Bay. We had been to Crisfield many times before; those trips had always been made by car from

in a direct line. Knowing the uncertainty of the wind, we desired to take every advantage that time could give us; hence an unusually early start. At first we had a fair wind, and plenty of it; it was right "astern" also. Before we reached the Great Wicomico, it was "dead ahead," and when we fairly opened the mouth of the Potomac there was a calm. This at first was simply an annoyance. We supposed it was merely one of the lulls we had so often experienced before, and endeavored to comfort ourselves by such philosophy. Hour after hour passed, but no wind came. The tide was carrying us down and across the bay,—just the direction we did not want to go. Then annoyance deepened into exasperation (senseless, to be sure), as the little yacht was tossed like a feather on the heavy swell. There was not a trace of air. Never before did I so fully realize what was meant by a dead calm. With each lurch of the boat the blocks creaked and the sails flapped heavily from side to side. The heat was more than the word intense implies; it was scorching, and the glare from the superheated deck was almost unendurable. What was the pleasure in yachting? None, under such circumstances. So that entire day passed. Exasperation gave place to,—well, call it fear. "All men are cowards at times," and it only renders matters worse to add to the weakness of fear the sin of prevarication.

All day the barometer had been going down. It was certain that a storm was impending. East, south, and west were filled with heavy clouds. We could hear the heavy thunder, and see the vivid lightning flash across the sky. Would there be enough of wind before the squall burst upon us to enable us to make some harbor? Or must we too stand the onset in our little boat out in the middle of the bay? These questions were never uttered, though I am quite sure they were inwardly asked by both Lew and myself.

Later in the afternoon a slight wind was seen coming over the water towards us from the mouth of the Potomac. It came so slowly that we feared it would die away before reaching us. After what appeared like an age it began to be felt, first fanning our cheeks, then filling our sails; and in a few minutes more we were

Slough boxes

our home port in St. Michaels. Whenever we announced that we were driving to Crisfield, we were met with the knowing response, "Going to have crabcakes at the Captain's Galley, are you?" There was no need to answer; after years of doing just that, our boatyard friends had come to know our ways.

We were awakened at five o'clock in the morning by the noise of our neighbors in the next slip, who were making happy preparations for a day of fishing. It was a crew of two fathers, each accompanied by a young son. They had discovered Mose the evening before and taken an immediate fancy to her. This morning they were sharing some of their breakfast with her. This turned out to be a good-sized piece of hamburger, which she promptly and proudly brought into the cabin, deposited in the middle of the rug, and began to eat. Rather more awake than I

quietly slipping through the water, back toward Great Wicomico, which we had passed early in the morning. This, to be sure, was not where we wanted to go, but choice was lost in thankfulness to reach any harbor. In two hours, just as darkness had fairly settled around us, we let our anchor go in a quiet arm of the Great Wicomico. It was a lovely, secluded little bay, in full sight of one of the greatest fishing establishments of the Chesapeake,—a perfect, "restful" place that we had found for the morrow, which was the Sabbath.

During the night the storm came; and, as we heard the wind whistling fiercely through the rigging, and felt the yacht rocking on the waves, we thought even kindly of the breeze which had carried us away from our destination, but into perfect safety.

I have related the experience of that day to show the most dismal side of yachting by sail. If one has a long purse and no end of generosity, if he is willing to keep a floating home for sailors, to be simply a passenger on his own boat, to go when and where his sailing-master directs, then a large steam-yacht is much better. I was yachting under other circumstances and with other objects in view; and, furthermore, as the season wore along, I gradually came to prefer risking my boat under my own directions than to accept what greater skill the presence of a sailing-master might bring. I will simply add: yacht-owner, learn the rudiments, go slowly, but command your own craft. If there be any manhood in the sport, that will bring it out. If there is not, then it were better abandoned.

On Monday, July the 2d, we were off, and with a stiff breeze astern soon passed the mouth of the Potomac. I do not know whether, or not, this river is usually treacherous, but as it so happened, that both of my friends, with whom I have conversed, and myself have been, as a rule, baffled there by the wind. By ten o'clock in the morning we were safely on the northern shore, and soon after two o'clock were at anchor back of Solomon's Island, in the Patuxent.

Patuxent may be called the dividing line between the low, sandy shore on the western side of the Chesapeake and the bolder

wished to be, I watched the remarkable daintiness with which she did this. She would pick up a chunk of the meat and shake pieces of it out of her mouth. Then she would select one delicate morsel after the next until every bit was gone. When she had finished, she began the washing up; whiskers and paws were meticulously groomed, whether in an attempt to find a last piece of hamburger or to achieve cleanliness only a cat knows. Finally finished, Mose leaped happily onto my bunk, scampering about, meowing impatiently when I didn't return a playful gesture. Ungraciously I buried my head under the pillow, hoping that if she couldn't see me, she would forget that I was there.

We spent the day lazily, giving in to the "leave the rush and hurry behind" mentality that grips all cruisers at some time during the journey. We sanded the handrails a little, scrubbed the decks, took a walk, and shopped in town, and the day was easily spent. We visited the Tawes Boating/Visitors Center and looked with enjoyment at the library and papers of former Governor J. Millard Tawes. Joseph T. Rothrock II had been the district forester for the Eastern Shore, and had come to know Millard Tawes as a friend, long before Tawes became the governor of Maryland. So again, the history of the Rothrocks and the Chesapeake Bay met in a path crossed by three generations.

On the following morning we woke early to the strong light of yet another fine day and departed the marina at six thirty. The jib was up, and a nice southeasterly wind aided us on our way up the Bay. As we passed the northern end of Smith Island, we again encountered numerous crab pots that required close vigilance at the helm and frequent slight course alterations. The visibility was unlimited; two hours out, we could still see the Crisfield tower on the horizon without using binoculars. We sailed past Marsh Island, past Deal Island, and entered Hooper Strait. Our course changed to 280 as we cut past the northern end of Bloodsworth Island. We had passed through miles of crab pots, some set in depths of fifty-four feet of water. On this calm, perfectly clear day, the pots made the waters ahead look like they were filled with apples put there for Halloween bobbing.

117

bluffs which we find more common on the upper parts of the bay. I have never seen a more beautiful illustration of how perfectly parallel to each other, strata may be deposited, and how subsequent erosion may remove some and leave other portions, than the northern shore of the Patuxent shows at the river's mouth and some distance inside and outside. Neither have I seen more tempting building-sites than these same bluffs offer. High, dry, fronting on salt water, with no fresh-water marshes near, such situations, one might infer, would be healthy. For aquatic sports the harbor of the Patuxent would offer abundant facilities. I have no doubt game is abundant both on land and on the water in season.

From the Patuxent we crossed to the Eastern Shore. Early in the morning there was a gentle breeze. It soon showed that we could not depend on it. I therefore headed directly across to secure an anchorage where we could hold what ground we had gained, and not drift hopelessly back with the tide. It was late in the afternoon before we had any wind. A large schooner that passed across our bow, going up the bay, had drifted back several miles astern of us. Night came on, dark enough, and we were obliged to appeal to the lead-line to aid us in finding our way up the Choptank, after passing the light off Benoni's Point. We at last, fearing to venture farther, let an anchor go in Lecompte's Bay on the southern shore of the Choptank. Next morning, July 4th, we had a fair wind into Cambridge Harbor.

Sunday morning, July 7th, I rose early, at half-past four. The pure glory of the morning impelled me to do so. Home-life is very apt to rob one of the cream of the day. Tired by the duties which the acquisition of daily bread imposes upon us, we shut ourselves within ourselves and brick walls. But this is not to be endured when yachting. The windows are widely open, and the earliest streak of dawn along the horizon invites you forth to receive your day's allowance of health fresh from the hand of morning. Some one says early risers are apt "to be conceited all forenoon and stupid all afternoon." This does not apply to one in whom the aquatic life has done its full work of regeneration. Constant in-

As we moved into Hooper Strait, we were surrounded by land. Sails down, under motor and autohelm, we were besieged by flies, of the biting variety. Joe tended the flyswatter, Mose flew about the cabin in a rapture of delight at so many moving targets to chase, and I got bit! For a full half hour Joe, arms moving as if he had been switched into fast-forward, swatted furiously until the head of the swatter flew off. At this critical moment, a course change provided us with some air. It was with comic relief that we looked at our headless swatter and decided that all Hooper Strait sailors should be provisioned with one swatter per crew member!

As we approached Hooper Island Light, we were heading west and the wind was blowing up out of the west. Recounting the many headwinds we had encountered, Joe was prompted to suggest that all cruises should be taken in reverse order in hopes of obtaining favorable wind conditions. When we wanted to sail up the Bay, the wind blew from the north. When we sailed south, there was a south wind against us. Such perversity can be annoying, but the openness and freedom of far horizons and wide skies more than make up for the less than accommodating wind.

Upon entering the Little Choptank, we began to see more sailboats. We also began to see the fins of swimming cow-nosed rays, and brought the boat around for a closer inspection. We were later told, by our friend Bryon, one of the owners of Higgins Yacht Yard in St. Michaels, whom we consider an authority on anything to do with boats and the Bay, that these were not of the dreaded stingray family. The reason we saw so many of these rays occurring so often in twos, was that they were mating. They are a benign species in terms of their sting, but not in their appearance—I would not want to swim among them.

The water was flat and smooth, reminding us more of a lake than an arm of the Chesapeake. We watched water skiers fly across its glassy surface and began to wonder if we ought to find a marina with an outlet for our fan. The only breeze going was the one we created as we motored along. Nonetheless, we yearned to anchor out; the idea of spending the night at a dock did not appeal to us this evening. As we began to look for a place to drop anchor, a

tercourse with nature has banished conceit, and when afternoon comes he does as most easy-going, sensible animals do,—deliberately goes to sleep and renews his stock of mental and physical vigor,—that is, if at anchor. If sailing, there can be no drowsiness by day or by night, short of absolute exhaustion. I am becoming each year less surprised at how little real good the majority of our health-seekers gain by their vacation. That they reap so little benefit, is simply, as a rule, because they have not earned it, and hence do not deserve it. The professional man, if he wants the vigor of the sailor who is with him, must do as the sailor does. One new muscular fibre is added to another, when by exercise we throw off the sloth-softened old ones.

When one can hardly keep his conscience quiet, when it reproaches him for making his vacation unduly long, then he is in a fair way to accomplish something notable on his return to duty. This sense of wasting time is often the best sign that vacation is doing a worthy and beneficent work. It tells how well the man has become, that he longs for activity in duty instead of longer rest.

The jelly-fish exist by thousands in portions of the Choptank. They fairly swarmed around the boat. But, graceful and wonderful as they were to watch, they were nonetheless a nuisance, inasmuch as the daily bath was often postponed because of them and their merited title, "sea-nettles." The mode of reproduction of these soft animals is wonderful, and when first fully made known sounded almost as strange as a fairy tale. It has, however, been written again and again, and is in every "Elementary Zoology"; so that we refrain from giving its details here.

The Choptank differs but little from the other rivers of the Chesapeake. Almost any one of them would afford a naturalist good working-ground for an entire season. There is, however, more monotony in the ground bordering the Choptank that in that along the Patuxent, for the former is nearly a dead level. Yet to me there is a quiet charm about the many-armed Choptank, which makes me wish to spend a whole vacation on its waters. During the season there is, *for those who care to catch them*, an abun-

slight breeze came up and we were heartened. Our good spirits were quickly dashed, however, as we explored Hills Point Cove; some sandbars that weren't indicated on our chart seemed to have reached up and grabbed us. As the first jolt hit us, we swung the tiller hard, but that seemed to push us farther aground. Our depthfinder continued to beep its warning, but refused to show us the way off. For a full half hour we were bumped aground before we could make ourselves free. As it was now seven thirty in the evening, we decided to abandon our present cove; around Ragged Island we found Brooks Creek, and dropped anchor just as the sun finished its work on this side of the earth. With the stars emerging as a twinkling canopy overhead, we ate a light supper and watched for shooting stars. As so often happened when we sat at night on our boat deck, we found ourselves looking outward, to the water and the world beyond. Thus we sat until sleepiness brought us back to ourselves; we had traveled sixty-one miles this day, and were ready to climb into our bunks.

The sun and an ever-playful Mose awakened us. We reviewed our charts over the breakfast table, and pulled anchor at eight o'clock. An anemometer reading gave the wind at 12 to 15 knots southwesterly; we headed for the Choptank on choppy seas. Joe, at the helm, was getting sprayed by the waves. He called to me, "Tell me how much fun I'm having." We were averaging a nice five knots until the wind took its morning break; we continued past Cork Point at a slower pace of three knots. We had read that NOAA was doing research work in this area of the Bay this summer for new chart development, although we did not sight any of the research buoys as we made our way.

In the light winds of the late morning, we ran our spinnaker up and picked up a couple of knots. Approaching Todd Point, we made radio contact with friends we had arranged to meet. This was part of the great fun of our cruise, and we were delighted to hear the voices of Jo Anne and Bob aboard the *Airborn*. Arranging with them for a later radio call, we headed past LeCompte Bay and Horn Point and sighted Cambridge. In summers gone by we had spent many pleasant days there either on the lawn of the yacht

Cambridge Harbor

dance of fish, crabs, and oysters. And during colder months water-fowl congregate there in vast numbers.

Cambridge may be taken as a characteristic town of the Eastern Shore. To those who have, as we had, friends there, it is always a most delightful place to visit. When we say that on the Eastern Shore one finds more of traces of the old colonial life and customs than elsewhere in Maryland, no disparagement is intended. On the contrary, we may be quite sure that the social habits and the hospitality, which form such striking reminders of earlier times, are real and most sincerely genuine, and are very certain to be impressed on the memory long after more formal meetings are forgotten.

There is certainly a great future awaiting the Eastern Shore. The climate, soil, and situation all combine to make one think that its rejuvenation cannot be long delayed. During the past few

Cambridge Harbor

club, or on a chase boat, watching the log canoe races and following the success of our favorite, the *Island Lark*, out of Higgins Yacht Yard. We've enjoyed Cambridge in other ways also. We've indulged in the pleasure of walking its brick-lined streets, viewing its eighteenth-century houses, and strolling through its park on craft festival days. Today, we viewed it as yachters, from the water, then came about and headed out to join our friends.

Anchored off the northern end of Bachelor Point, we met the *Airborn* and went for an afternoon swim. In five and a half feet of water, with a sandy bottom and no jelly fish, we frolicked and recounted our past month's adventure. Bob and Jo Anne took turns on the windsurfer, breezing along with skill and finesse. Joe, an excellent swimmer and sailor, had tried his hand at the sport, having what we called "unidirectional success." He was able to go or to come with ease; turning around was another story. With

123

years the new industry of oyster-canning has given some towns a most extraordinary impetus. I do not regard this, as it is now conducted, as likely to be of any great, permanent good, because it must require but a few years to remove the oysters on which present prosperity depends, unless oyster-raising becomes, as it may, a feasible thing. To this we shall allude later. But when I remember the agricultural capacity of the Eastern Shore I think its future is certain, simply because the rest of the country "hath need of it." I am convinced that in the next generation the owner of land on the Eastern Shore will be said to have, like the owner of a rich silver-mine in the West, "a sure thing."

The yacht left Cambridge on the morning of July 9th,—that was just before the peaches were ripe. Hence we were prevented from seeing the shipment of the great peninsular crop. Peach season is, of all times, the one in which to visit the region. More information can be gained then than at any other time.

We could notice a great change in the weather since we went down the bay a month earlier. Then the wind appeared to be continuous, or usually so, in one direction from early in the morning until towards evening. When we left Cambridge we found that the calms we had experienced off the mouth of the Potomac and in crossing from the Patuxent to the Eastern Shore were but the first of a series. From Cambridge up, we were reasonably sure of a morning breeze (though often a very gentle one), then a noon-day calm, then more or less threatening weather towards evening. Not that evening always brought its squall, for it did not, but that it nearly always attempted to,—if such an expression be allowable.

Starting from Cambridge at 9 A.M with a fair breeze, which died out, it was a full twelve hours before we dropped our anchor in the snug little harbor between Poplar Island and the main-land. I was particularly anxious for a good, rousing wind that day, as my friend, Captain Thomas Howard, was with me, and I wanted to show my little sloop to the best advantage. When we stopped for

chagrin, he would fall off, turn the board the way he intended to go, climb back on, pick up the sail, and do well until he had to come about again. Jo Anne's children, Katie and John, discovered Mose looking over the stern and quickly gave up swimming to play with her. As late afternoon turned to early evening, we boarded our boats and headed into Oxford. There, we found a slip and met some cruising friends of Bob's and Jo Anne's.

We spent the next day in and around Oxford. The weather continued to be hot, humid, and hazy. After dinner we noted that the clouds we had been watching throughout the afternoon had darkened the sky to a blue-black color. The weather was typical of that before a storm. From the safety of the marina, we watched as the lightning that heralds an approaching storm forked the sky. A light rain started to fall but no thunder was heard. Huddled under the protection of our dodger with our friends, we recounted an incredible experience we had had the year before in Annapolis.

That summer, we had met friends in Annapolis for the weekend and anchored off City Dock. We had taken our dinghy ashore for dinner, and were strolling with ice-cream cones when raindrops prompted us to return quickly to our boats. As we did so, the rain stopped. Back on board, we wondered if we had acted precipitously when the lightning began. The lightning was from a distant storm and no thunder accompanied it. It zigzagged across the sky, branching at each change of direction. It flashed with spectacular brilliance. Out in the harbor, what had been silent concern turned into amazed delight; oohs and aahs could be heard from our fellow boaters as we watched impressive, beautiful patterns. After a particularly striking trail blazed over them, people began to clap; it was like a Fourth of July fireworks display without the booms to announce the celebration. It ended abruptly, without any more rain, and we began quiet discussions about the remarkable powers of nature; we had been frightened, then inspired and moved to applause in the span of only a few minutes.

the night, it was blowing hard from the south. The last two or three miles of our run were made before a wind under which the yacht fairly staggered; and as we passed over the shoal water in the darkness, before reaching our anchorage, I knew that if we made any mistake and ran aground, the mast would go like a reed in a hurricane. In spite of the wind, which whistled through the rigging, we lay down in a most comfortable frame of mind. We could feel the boat tugging away at the anchor, but having full confidence in the strength of our cable and in the holding power of the anchor, we could sleep undisturbed.

Leaving Poplar Island next morning, we threaded our way out into the bay past the southern end of Kent Island. It should be here stated that a light-house has been erected within a few years on the end of the bar which "makes out" from the southern point of Kent. Outside of that bar is one of the deepest parts of the bay. My chart shows, for a single point there, eighteen fathoms.

From Kent Island across to Annapolis our run was short and pleasant. We reached our old anchorage there just about noon. After dinner we went to the top of the State-house. When the gentlemanly janitor accorded us this privilege, it was with the proviso that we should not use our pencils or knives on the building. Apart from the fact that we had no desire to leave any kind of memorial of our visit, was the further fact that we could not have done so if we had so desired, as previous visitors had already covered the dome with their scribbling. Adventurous, ambitious fellows had climbed, at the risk of their bones and lives, up under the timbers of the dome, and there marked or carved their names. Who can fathom the depth of human vanity? The desire for such notoriety implies the lurking suspicion that some one will care to read the inscription. As a rule, the less the importance of the scribbler the greater the desire for such immortality. To return to the dome, however. Such a panorama as we had there spread out below us is seldom to be seen. The country was looking its very best. The reaped and the promised crops bespoke the fertility of the soil, just as the throng of small boats engaged in fishing, told how prolific the water was. Undulating hills, with valleys through

The next morning, clouds veiled the sun in Oxford, and the rain was still falling. It didn't dampen our spirits; there is a pleasant tradition among yachters to maintain a holiday mood regardless of the weather. Bob and Jo Ann departed first; the rain might have been solely arranged for them, if only as an excuse to don new raingear. An hour later they radioed to tell us they had good winds with a broad reach all the way.

We headed out under morning skies that were still shrouded in grey, and there was a decided chill in the June air. Many times before we had started with gloomy weather forecasts marking the beginning of a day that turned out rather decently at the end; this day was to be no exception.

A couple of hours later we were in the channel approaching Knapps Narrows. We had been on a steady starboard tack, with no complaints about the wind although the weather continued to be chilly. We took on diesel fuel at the Knapps Narrows Marina, and saw that the clouds in the sky were showing signs of breaking up. Past Buoy #1 on our way out of the channel, an osprey, chee-ing loudly at us, picked up an eel from its nest, and, prey dangling from its beak, circled the nest until we were safely past. Thereupon, it returned to the nest, where another osprey sat waiting to share the meal. Looking up to watch the ospreys, we saw little patches of blue showing through the clouds.

Soon we were passing Poplar Island. A warm breeze was now blowing, and we changed into shorts. We looked carefully, trying to imagine the *Martha* anchored in the circle of islands that enclose the bay. Now the islands are owned by the Smithsonian Institution, and osprey are encouraged to nest there. We do not know if many boaters anchor there, for it is quite unprotected.

By the time we reached Annapolis, warm sunshine sparkled on the water and our white mainsail was framed against a lovely blue sky. We reached the marina, joined our friends for the evening, and spoke of the other evenings we had had away from our home port on this cruise. We could not help but think about other trips we had made and the sense of homecoming that pervades the

which navigable streams ran, made a perfect lowland landscape. Mountains near, or even remote but visible, might have made a *stronger* picture, though they could have added nothing to the calm, peaceful perfection of that landscape. I could have studied and enjoyed it day after day without weariness.

The evening of the 11th of July found us in the Chester River, after a most wearisome drift across and up the bay. About 4 P.M. dark clouds came up in the south, and, anticipating a blow, we lowered away our sail to take in a double reef. This was hardly done before the squall was upon us. In a few minutes we had, for the river, very high waves, and, more than all, found that we had a lee-shore much nearer than we liked. However, the vessel carried her sail well, and we "clawed off" in good style.

Queenstown, in the southern bend of the river, was where we decided to anchor for the night. We succeeded, after getting aground, in working our way into the little harbor through a provokingly narrow channel. The names of the towns on the Eastern Shore are strikingly suggestive of Old England: Queenstown, Oxford, Cambridge, Easton, Chester, all indicate pride in, and affection for, the mother-country.

Sometimes for weeks the yachtsman has to do almost constantly with calm or squall, and the alternatives narrow down to drifting or scudding. We apparently had entered upon one of those trying periods. As we came out of Chester River, there was a bare suspicion of wind. No one could say where it came from,— first south, then west, then nowhere. After exercise of great patience and muscle we had worked, by 3 P.M., out into the bay again. Meanwhile, the clouds were piling up dark and threatening, and the falling barometer told that beyond doubt a storm was impending. Together with these, there were obvious warnings,— there was a peculiar, hazy atmosphere and an absolute stillness— which led us to think that when it did come, it would be severe. The cloud-bank moved, from the southeast, west, then toward the north, gathering, as it went, into a heavy, blue-gray or lead-colored (but not black) mass. There is something in waiting for such an onset not unlike the feeling with which the soldier waits

conclusion of each voyage. We were only a few days out of St.
Michaels now. The pleasurable anticipation of going home is
different somehow when a trip has been made by boat. In a
strange city, there is, with the onset of darkness, a sense of a
community withdrawing behind its lighted windows. We found
that a new port at night has its shadows and silences, but these are
punctuated by voices and laughter, sometimes heard close by,
sometimes at a distance. There seems to be an inherent group
loyalty among boaters, a willingness to share pleasures and interests with each other. Perhaps we felt it more acutely because it
fit into our desire of making this cruise special, given our warm
association with great-grandfather and the past. We sat in the
darkness with friends and contemplated the scenes near our
journey's end.

The thing we wanted to do most on this visit to Annapolis was to
get into the dome of the State House. We learned from the
building superintendent, Mr. Paul Woods, that the dome was a
"secure area," closed for some years now to the general public.
But Mr. Woods and Security Chief Major Symms were gracious
enough to hear our story and make an exception in our case,
thereby enabling us to retrace great-grandfather's steps. We were
led through roped off areas, locked doors, of which there were
quite a few, onto an ancient gilt and grilled elevator whose brass
and wood panels were shining with care, and finally to an ascent of
413 narrow wooden steps. I began to understand why the public
was forbidden; my legs ached, and I was totally incapable of
speech by the time we arrived at the top, not from wonder, but
from breathlessness!

Through the final locked door, and there before us was Annapolis, spreading out in crooked, diverging avenues. Round the
parapet we went, watching the sun bounce off the water on one
side, filling our field of vision with the panorama of historic
buildings and cobblestone streets that make Annapolis such a
delight for the tourist. Being on the top of the dome made us feel
like we were somehow at the focus of the town, with the State

for the enemy's charge. It was certain to come, and it was certain to be full of danger. Those who can best control their feelings are the most fortunate. The man who under such circumstances boasts that he has no fear is not so much to be envied for his supposed fortitude as pitied for his lack of truthfulness.

There was a large schooner which came out of the river with us. She had headed northward for Baltimore, and we were endeavoring to enter the Magothy River, to the west. First we saw the schooner take down her topsail, then her foresail, then her jib, then her mainsail. We knew that there was no time to waste. It was evident that the captain, looking to the windward, had reason for his prompt action. So we lowered our jib and put a double reef in our mainsail. We had hoped to carry enough of canvas to run into Magothy River. The bay was still as calm as a mill-pond after we had shortened sail. But in a few minutes, darkness suddenly shut the schooner to the north of us out from view. In an instant later the rush of wind was upon us. The stanch little boat endured the tremendous strain so bravely that we were at once reassured as to her seaworthiness; and she held her way toward the harbor. "Mose" braced himself against the tiller, and, though a powerful man, it required all his strength to keep the boat from luffing, as her jib was down. In less than five minutes the waves were breaking over us, and spray dashed into our faces until we were no longer able to endure it. If we could have stood at our posts, the boat would have gone safely into the Magothy River. But we could not, and there was nothing left for us to do, except to lower the mainsail and go to the southward, under bare poles, before the wind. This had become the more necessary as we were now among larger vessels, all of which were scudding. Hence, if for no other reason than to keep out of their way, we were obliged to do likewise.

The intensity of the wind did not last more than twenty minutes; but while it did last our speed was fearful. To make matters worse, we were towing the yawl-boat, which ran up on to us and would drive its iron-clad bow into the stern of the yacht

From the State House dome

House sitting looming in the center, soft clouds ringing its horizon, casting its symbolic shadow over all it guarded.

On the way back down, we were equally as excited, as we explored the broad, hand hewn beams that were the repository of the signatures of visitors that great-grandfather had seen on his visit. We were impressed with the ornateness of some of the signatures, written and carved with flourishes and flair. We mused about the aspirations and hopes of those who had immortalized themselves in wood. Out on the street, we gazed up at where we had so recently walked. Golden and shining, the dome rose up, steadfast and unchanging.

Across and up the Bay, we made our way into Queenstown. We had been here many times before, enjoying its snug harbor with different boating friends. In the early evening we watched a

with tremendous force. As the darkness "lifted," we saw coming down astern of us a large schooner. To keep out of its way, the jib was hoisted. It was impossible to prevent the yacht from "yawing" when she rose on the waves, and then the jib would fly from side to side until each time the sheet tightened it made our heavy bowsprit quiver like a reed. Soon after, we hoisted the peak of the mainsail. We soon saw that there was no danger now so long as we kept going before the wind, for, in spite of the high seas which had followed us, not a drop of water came on board after we headed south. The buoyancy of the boat was wonderful. And, from that day forth, I felt that my yacht more than compensated for being slower than some others, by being safer. The iron ballast, low down and well fastened, evidently, was just where it was doing the most good.

In an hour it was all over; and, under sail, we were heading for Annapolis Harbor. We could now look around and see the damage done by the squall. Several vessels, whose sails had been split, were repairing damages. Others, like ourselves, were hunting an anchorage. Just as the sun went down we dropped anchor in the same snug berth that we had left two days before.

Looking back on this squall, I can now only regard it as a small cyclone,—at least, having its revolving character. Before it disappeared the clouds were again back in the south. The rain, though heavy, was not in proportion to the wind.

Viewing these storms, after several seasons of cruising, I am more than ever surprised that a good barometer is not regarded as an essential part of every vessel's outfit. I am safe in asserting that mine never once deceived me during all the time I had been using it, and that it has often put me in a safe position by its timely warning. Once, indeed, taking advantage of its indications, we sought shelter through a gale which strewed the bay with wrecks, and which cost many human lives within a few miles of where we lay in quiet. It may appear like a waste of words to urge this subject, but, knowing many yachting-parties never include this instrument among their effects, I wish to say that when I claim

Inside the dome

boat come in; it caught our interest because, standing half out of
the forward hatch, a lovely Siamese seemingly was keeping watch
for a good place to drop anchor. With the wooded shore as a
backdrop, this elegant cat stood sleek and heedless of the exclamations of those who saw her. Eyes fixed on the waters ahead, she
posed in wooden stillness, an unmoving silhouette. The boat
quietly made its way into the creek, taking its mascot out of our
view. Later, we dinghied into the town dock to take a short walk.
In the past, we would often be accompanied by friends who
jogged along the streets; we are saunterers, and preferred a
leisurely stroll. It would be fair to say, actually, that leisurely is the
perfect word to describe all of our activities as boaters; we are
never caught up in the rush to get somewhere. That is quite what
we love most about boating. We have enough of hurrying and

small vessels may undertake long voyages, I only do so when this instrument is on board and all the due precautions have been taken. Anything short of this is simple foolhardiness, which nothing can justify or extenuate.

The day after the squall we started again to go up the bay. Leaving Annapolis early in the morning, the breeze, though ahead of us, was promising enough, so far as its strength was concerned, but on our very first tack it died away entirely, and we drifted hopelessly. About two o'clock it revived just a little, and we headed for Magothy River. By dint of hard rowing, we at last rounded Sandy Point, and then reached the mouth of the river. Then turning south into Deep Creek, we anchored for the night. For small craft, a more desirable haven than this could not be well found. Later in the evening I discovered that the water was as well stocked with pickerel as the shore was with wood-ticks. The channel had from six to eight feet of water in it, but along-shore it was shallow and muddy.

The chief productions of the region appeared to be melons, peaches, and "garden truck." Proximity to Baltimore doubtless made such interests very lucrative there. The busy freighting-season for these productions was just coming on, and it was with difficulty that I convinced one farmer that I could not be induced to do his carrying for him.

The morning of July 14th was clear, and gave no indication, by barometer or otherwise, of an impending storm. By 5 A.M. we were well started,—that is, in the absence of the wind we went out, like Barkis, "with the tide." But we were no sooner in the bay than a nice breeze sprang up. It bore promise on its wings, for it was none of those puffy winds which we had felt so often before, but a steady, constantly strengthening one that intimated its full intention of remaining with us for the day. It increased as the sun rose. Before ten o'clock, however, dark clouds were in the west, and the barometer gave undoubted signs of a coming storm. As far as we could see to the south the vessels were "holding the wind." This encouraged us to think that this same friendly breeze would last until we reached Still Pond Harbor before the storm came.

meeting of deadlines in our professional lives, and thus have discarded that part of it when we are on our boat.

Back on board, we considered how lovely an anchorage Queenstown makes, no matter how many times the boater visits it. Here, whenever the mariner seeks its harbor, is a secluded, tree lined resting place.

We left the Chester River and headed for our home port of St. Michaels. We would make the trip back to the Chesapeake and Delaware Canal, as great-grandfather had, at another time, for we did not quite have the luxury that he had had in scheduling ourselves away from our jobs. At the yacht yard there were friends to greet us and messages from other boating friends who were coming in to join us for the weekend. Thus it was that we found ourselves over at the Miles River Yacht Club with the Follweilers, who had sailed in from Tolchester, and the next evening up the Wye River with Jan and Pam White, from St. Michaels, and Pat and Aaron Blumberg, who had sailed in from Chestertown. It was good to have gone cruising and just as good to be back at an anchorage with our friends. Everyone met Mose, promptly fell in love with her, and just as promptly wanted to know, "How was it?"

How it was is how it is for every Chesapeake Bay sailor. It is a beautiful body of water to sail, at times looking like the painted flat of a stage set. Unhurried, there were no marching lines of houses, no tenements, no suburban stretches with gravel and smoke and abandoned cars. We saw and experienced life on the water, which is the side of life cared about and treasured by all boaters. Anyone who has ever cast off, even if only in a dinghy, knows something of how it was. Pleasure in the challenge, in the closeness that sailing brings, in the serenity of one's surroundings—all of those things we found. The *Response*, so named because she is obedient to her helm, had taken us into quiet places and to festivals, all in the same month, with weather that was nearly perfect. All of this gave us abundant reason for remembering the trip with pleasure.

We had come back from our trip on the Chesapeake renewed and inspired by great-grandfather's achievements. In the month

Swan Point was left behind us, and in a couple of hours we passed
Worton's Creek; then we rounded the point and stood in for Still
Pond. We had the usual difficulty getting over the bar, and
working through the narrow inlet to the pond. But we succeeded,
and by one o'clock we had two anchors out and sails all snugly
stowed. Then we went below,—"Mose" to preparing dinner, and
we to preparing for an "afternoon fish" after the storm was over.
So far as the ordinary dangers of navigation were concerned, we
had passed out of them when we entered our harbor. It was
astonishing to see how little impression the wind made on the boat
where she lay; but, looking outside, we could see others tossing
furiously on the waves. The rain was severe, and the wind too,
though the latter was nothing like that of two days before. During
the afternoon we had a succession of thunder-storms. The play of
the lightning was very grand. Both zigzag and sheet lightning
illuminated the heavens. As we watched, we could see tall spires
and ruined buildings, even, represented in the fiery shapes on the
sky. Afloat or ashore, it matters not: man lives more during an
hour of storm than during any other equal period. His own utter
weakness and the unlimited power of the elements, both, force
themselves upon his mind. There is no escape from either. He
need not be an abject, cringing coward to realize both to the
fullest extent. On the contrary, he may be a brave man, and one
full of good faith and of good deeds, and still these feelings will rise
and overwhelm him. A thunder-storm is a rich experience,—one
well worth living through.

On our way up from Magothy we met the "John McClintock
Yacht Club," bound down the bay. As they were from Philadelphia, we could not refrain from saluting them, though our vessel
was very diminutive alongside of theirs. The salute was returned
in the most cordial and gentlemanly manner. Wishing each other
a successful voyage, we held our courses and were soon out of
sight. These yachting-parties, where congenial friends hire a good
vessel and at a minimum of expense get a maximum of rational
recreation, are becoming much more frequent. They are also
creating a just public sentiment in favor of aquatic sports. There

that we journeyed, we had felt the presence of the man who had
had the fortitude to navigate the Bay and its rivers and coves with
the sailing competence to achieve a complete cruise. We increas-
ingly admired the words with which he articulated his experiences, enabling us to have a very real sense of what they were like.
When we began our venture into the past, we felt a little like
people who love gardens without knowing everything they would
like to about the plants growing there. Guided on our way with
great-grandfather's ship's log and book, we were able to place
modern sites in their historical context. We began to see with
more sensitive eyes the natural beauty of the Chesapeake, captur-
ing our visits and stops with light meter and lens, to preserve them
forever. Our month-long voyage was not simply a piece of sailing;
it was an experience. Saint Exupéry's *The Little Prince* immor-
talizes for us our feelings about this experience. In that beautiful
fable the Prince learns that the rose and the fox are nothing until
someone has tamed them, making them friends. Once this hap-
pens the friends become unique, and are seen through the heart
and not the eyes—thus, this cruise was committed to the memory
of our hearts.

was a time, not many years ago, when to be a yachtsman was entirely synonymous with being a blackguard, in the eyes of many well-thinking persons; and, to tell the truth, this imputation was too often deserved. He who wrote "Rob Roy on the Jordan" did missionary work, both when he distributed tracts and alms among the poverty-stricken souls, and when he sailed in his little yacht,—no less in the one case than in the other. He preached salvation to soul and body both.

Darkness came on at Still Pond before the net was placed as we desired. Though the next morning, one twenty-inch pickerel showed that during the month between our first and second visits to the place the supply had not been exhausted.

There are fated spots, sailors think. I never, save once, have gone from Still Pond to the mouth of the Elk that I did not have to drift, or, at most, to sail with barely enough of wind to give us "steerage-way." My last trip up, over the same water, was no exception. Hour after hour the bay was undisturbed by any breeze whatever. Our only comfort lay in the fact, well known to sailors, that some boats drift better than others and we had the satisfaction of being among the best in that kind of navigation. Later at night, on July 15th, we anchored in Elk River,—still in sight of our starting-point in the morning. The rising sun of the following day brought with it a moderate breeze, before which we made our way through Back Creek to Chesapeake City.

In spite of its storms and its calms, its over-dreaded mosquitoes, and its alleged malaria, I haved come to think of the Chesapeake Bay as my sanitarium. I know that I come back from my trips there stronger than when I start on them. It is a soul-expanding process simply to gaze out on the water, to study the features of the headlands, and to conjecture in what time and by what agencies they were formed.